Simple Living:
being content with enough

David Watson

Help for the journey…

First published in Great Britain, January 2023
www.GileadBooksPublishing.com

Copyright © Anne Watson 2023

British Library Cataloguing-in-Publication Data:
A catalogue record for this book is available from the British Library.
ISBN-13: 978-1-8381828-4-7

All rights reserved.
No part of this publication may be reproduced, stored in a retrieval system or transmitted in any form or by any means, electronic, mechanical, photocopying, recording or otherwise, without the prior permission of the publisher.

Unless otherwise indicated all Scripture quotations are taken from THE HOLY BIBLE, NEW INTERNATIONAL VERSION®, NIV® Copyright © 1973, 1978, 1984, 2011 by Biblica, Inc.® Used by permission. All rights reserved worldwide.
Scripture quotations marked (JB) are taken from the JERUSALEM BIBLE Copyright© 1966, 1967, 1968 by Darton, Longman & Todd LTD and Doubleday and Co. Inc. All rights reserved.
The publisher makes every effort to ensure that the papers used in our books are made from trees that have been legally sourced from well-managed and credibly certified forests by using a printer awarded FSC & PEFC chain of custody certification.

Compiled from sermons and talks given at different stages of David's ministry. These have been edited and updated by the publisher.

Front cover image credit: Rufar/AdobeStock

CONTENTS

1. Rich Christians in an Age of Hunger	5
I am certainly not rich	9
We don't have a Lazarus at our back door	13
The well-off members of our community need Christ just as much as others	15
2. The Simplicity of Jesus	24
A call to urgency	26
A call to unity	32
A call to humility	36
A call to simplicity	40
A call to sensitivity	47
A call to reality	50
A call to certainty	53
3. The Four 'Musts'	59
We must accept frustration over giving and sharing	65
We must aim at life and not just at generous charity	67
We must go on working on this theme	70
We must take some action	73
4. You Cannot Lose	75
God is on the side of the poor	75
God identifies with the poor	78

God works through the poor 83
God wants us to concentrate more on the poor 88
God is no one's debtor 91

5. Simple Living 93
It was a gift of love 97
It was a gift of faith 101
It was a gift of herself 107

6. Q&As 111
1. Is it right or wrong to save? 111
2. What about helping those suffering in our own country? 115
3. Responding to local needs 117
4. How do I balance saving time and saving money? 120
5. Is the value of a secular job just to support others for fulltime Christian work? 123
6. Aren't we getting too "good works-orientated" by focussing on giving and the needs of the developing world? 127
7. Where can we send the money? 128
8. Is giving money to developing countries really the answer? 129
9. Shouldn't we try to change the structures of society? 129

Chapter 1
Rich Christians in an Age of Hunger

"There was a rich man who was dressed in purple and fine linen and lived in luxury every day. At his gate was laid a beggar named Lazarus, covered with sores and longing to eat what fell from the rich man's table. Even the dogs came and licked his sores.

"The time came when the beggar died and the angels carried him to Abraham's side. The rich man also died and was buried. In Hades, where he was in torment, he looked up and saw Abraham far away, with Lazarus by his side. So he called to him, 'Father Abraham, have pity on me and send Lazarus to dip the tip of his finger in water and cool my tongue, because I am in agony in this fire.'

"But Abraham replied, 'Son, remember that in your lifetime you received your good things, while Lazarus received bad things, but now he is comforted here and you are in agony. And besides all this, between us and you a great chasm has been set in place, so that those who want to go *from here to you cannot, nor can anyone cross over from there to us.'*

"He answered, 'Then I beg you, father, send Lazarus to my family, for I have five brothers. Let him warn them, so that they will not also come to this place of torment.'

"Abraham replied, 'They have Moses and the Prophets; let them listen to them.'

"'No, father Abraham,' he said, 'but if someone from the dead goes to them, they will repent.'

"He said to him, 'If they do not listen to Moses and the Prophets, they will not be convinced even if someone rises from the dead.'" Luke 16:19-31

Last Monday evening I flew into Malta in the midst of a Cyclone. The wind was 55mph and we were told later on that 100-year-old trees were just pulled up by their roots, roofs had been torn off and the flight controller, who was on duty at the time said, when we met him, that he never thought we would ever get down in one piece! It was quite an experience so thank you very much indeed for praying for the visit. This evening as we read from Acts 27, we were reminded that the Apostle Paul also had a rough time when he came into Malta 2000 years ago.

Last November, however, a wind of twice that force, about 100mph, whipped up a wave about twenty feet high and tore into South India for a distance of twenty miles. Within minutes 85,000 people were killed, 2 million people were homeless, crops destroyed, cattle perished, and tens of thousands of children became orphaned within minutes. Perhaps we've almost forgotten the details of that disaster, because we gave an offering before Christmas and so easily these things fade from our minds. Perhaps we've even thought that in parts of the world disaster and poverty are so common, so much almost a way of life, that possibly they are able to accept it philosophically. Can they?

Ernest Oliver an associate director of Tear Fund and someone who has been a missionary in India for 25 years once said, "I cannot recall a single person, who was contented with what they had, each one was constantly in a battle to improve their situation, not one was satisfied with being poor, with not having a proper meal a day, with the perpetual insecurity of not having anything to eat the next day, not one was content with being weak and sick or at the prospect of losing their babies soon after birth. Their Asian philosophy had not made them indifferent to suffering.

It is perhaps against this kind of harsh reality of life which was all too common in the New Testament and also too common today in many parts of the world that Jesus told one of his most disturbing and most challenging parables that you will find anywhere in the gospel.

Two men, one rich, one poor, we often call them Dives and Lazarus. One day both died. Lazarus went to heaven and Dives to hell and there was no way by which one could cross to the other side after death. A great chasm was fixed, as Jesus put it.

Now the story is well known, but what may not be so well known is that by the rich man, Jesus was not thinking about some Godless millionaire cruising around Malta in his yacht. He was almost certainly thinking of a decent, respectable religious man, enjoying the sort of affluence that most of us enjoy here today and in the West in general. Not necessarily very wealthy at all by some standards, but extremely comfortable when compared with those utterly destitute. For example in verse 19, the rich man is described as clothed in purple and fine linen and I am sure Jesus chose those particular words because they happen to describe the robes of a High Priest, and if you look at verse 14, because the context is always important in any parable, the Pharisees, Luke says, who were lovers of money, heard all this and they scoffed at him. That is the context of this story of Dives and Lazarus, as a religious man might well have tithed everything he possessed perhaps he put five pounds, ten pounds every Sunday in the offering. A very religious, prayerful, devout, respectable man but still very comfortable when compared with poor sick Lazarus.

If you are anything like me, you may find it incredibly easy to rationalize the challenge which comes through the plight of the poor in the world at this moment. Let me mention some of the excuses that I expect everyone of us here, without exception, has made from time to time when we have before us this kind of challenge.

I AM CERTAINLY NOT RICH

"I am on a student loan, I am mortgaged up to the hilt, I can't even get a job. I am a poor..." A couple were working out whether they could afford to get married.

"Darling, said one of the couple, I think I can live on your salary, but what are you going to live on?"

I certainly know that several of you in this congregation are very hard up indeed, that you are finding it extremely difficult to pay your bills. It is not easy at all and I know that there are a number of people who are far from well off, and I am thrilled when I hear of money flowing more and more freely within the fellowship from A to B and from B to C, as it needs to happen and it needs to happen much more. We are one family; we belong to one another. If we know of a need somewhere we need to be able to give freely, both of money and possessions or whatever it is so that we really care for one another, that's what love means in a fellowship here or anywhere else.

Tell me how many here live on less than £900 a year. Well, you are better off than a quarter of the world's population, 1.9 billion people[1] and remember that the

---

[1] The World Bank, OCTOBER 17, 2018, PRESS RELEASE NO 2019/044/DEC-GPV, https://www.worldbank.org/en/news/press-release/2018/10/17/nearly-half-the-world-lives-on-less-than-550-a-day

destitute are not happy, they are not content with their poverty. Again, how many here have eaten absolutely nothing today and are not likely to eat tomorrow either. 815 million people are starving at this moment [2] and tens of millions of children suffer irreversible brain damage because of malnutrition. Their families have no money for the simplest of healthy diets. How many of us here have eaten beef, pork or chicken today? Reports suggest that livestock in rich counties such as ours eat nearly 40% of the world's grain, rather than it being fed to hungry people.[3]

On wider issues where we must bear corporate responsibility in the West, the financial assistance we give from this country to all the poor countries is 0.7% of our gross national income.[4] Yet we clamour for more and more wages all the time.

---

[2] World Vision 18 March 2018 https://www.worldvision.org/hunger-news-stories/global-hunger-facts
[3] http://news.cornell.edu/stories/1997/08/us-could-feed-800-million-people-grain-livestock-eat
[4] https://fullfact.org/economy/uk-foreign-aid-budget-what-did-government-spend-2017/ In 2021 the UK Government

Again, the USA spends 3.5% of its gross national income on military spending [5] and less than 1% on foreign aid.[6] In fact, each American spends more on sweets than the US government gives per person on development aid.[7] And back in this country the money we spend each year on slimming tablets and slimming food, notice the word slimming, is roughly £2 billion, the same as we spend on humanitarian aid throughout the world.[8]

In what sense are we not the rich man in this parable? Compared with about a thousand million people we eat sumptuously, every day.

reduced the UK aid budget to 0.5% GNI as a 'temporary measure' following the global pandemic
[5] $623 billion, https://edition.cnn.com/2018/07/11/politics/trump-defense-spending/index.html
[6] https://politicsofpoverty.oxfamamerica.org/2017/04/7-things-didnt-know-about-us-foreign-assistance/
[7] http://s3.amazonaws.com/blog.oxfamamerica.org/politicsofpoverty/2017/04/ForeignAid101_summary-2017-v2.png
[8] https://www.independent.co.uk/voices/comment/52-is-just-the-latest-britain-s-diet-industry-is-worth-2-billion-so-why-do-we-buy-into-it-8737918.html
https://fullfact.org/economy/uk-spending-foreign-aid/

WE DON'T HAVE A LAZARUS AT OUR BACK DOOR

"If we did of course, we would give him something to eat we wouldn't think twice about it." The trouble today is that Lazarus is not at our back door, he is in our very living room. He comes to us online, via the television, on the radio, in our newspapers, he is inescapable. I have here a copy of Tear Times and the picture is of a poor man, and it's the kind of picture we have seen some thousands and thousands of times over. A former member of this church, some years ago, who is now working with the South American Mission Society in Peru, wrote in his Christmas Newsletter these two stories. "I was on my way home from taking the children to school when I saw him. There he was poking through the rubbish looking for something that might be useful. It was not the first time that I had seen him. A few weeks earlier I had spotted him nearer our home, poking through the rubbish in the hope that he could find something to eat. He is a man of about sixty years of age, and this is his regular occupation, going round to see what the better off had discarded so that he might gain something with which to survive, I would not use the word live, survive is better. But what really hit hard is that he is part of our church."

"Another house around the corner three little girls ran out. "Where is your brother?" I asked. "Gone to look for work" they replied. "Your Mother?" "She's gone to look for work too" Then the younger one says, "We have nothing in the house to eat today" an older sister said, "We did not eat yesterday, either". Again, this is a family connected with our church.

And it's not just the church in Peru because that church is our church. There's only one church. There is only one body of Christ. There is only one spiritual family, God's family.

If I had gone without food for a couple of days because I couldn't afford something I know you would do something about it, and I would do it for you too. But these are our family, and of the 811 million[9] who are starving today, faceless people as far as we are concerned, very many of them are our brothers and sisters in Christ. Quite apart from the responsibility we have to share God's love with those who are not yet in Christ but are still made in the image of Christ.

---

[9] https://www.wfp.org/publications/hunger-map-2021

THE WELL-OFF MEMBERS OF OUR COMMUNITY NEED CHRIST JUST AS MUCH AS OTHERS

I would agree that there are the up and outs as well as the down and outs. Everyone without Christ is in desperate need. Therefore, the argument goes that we must keep up a certain standard of living otherwise we will never communicate with them, never be able to win them for Christ. How easy it is to argue like that when it comes to the clothes we wear, the food we eat, the furniture we buy and the things we do. But if you and I take that line of argument, we must then ask ourselves some straight questions. How much of my affluent lifestyle is honestly related to witnessing to my rich and affluent friends and neighbours? How much has it honestly helped to bring any to Christ? Do the quality of my clothes, my food, my drinks, my furniture etc, really help others in any way to see the love and reality of Christ? Are those who are gripped by the materialistic values in life, honestly convinced of our faith in Christ, when outwardly we seem to have exactly the same materialistic values as they do?

The playwright and screenwriter Murray Watts put it like this, in a very powerful remark. "The world is increasingly deaf to a church that is sold out to materialism, it is only when the world is confronted by the church as a beggar, spiritually and materially destitute, dependent wholly upon God's provisions that any impact will be made." It is tragic when the church takes its colour from the world, and it can only lead to great bitterness, directed against religion.

We need to remember that God's supreme communication of himself was in his own son Jesus Christ, who for our sake became poor. Not poverty stricken, but poor and he certainly communicated it. When Christians down the years have followed the lifestyle of their Master, they have always enhanced and never hindered, their witness to Jesus Christ.

An obvious example of this would be Mother Teresa of Calcutta. In a fascinating book by Malcolm Muggeridge, called "Christ and the Media"[10] he said that Mother Teresa's appearance on television was one of the very few supremely successful Christian programmes. Why? Because: "The total dedication of her life showed through the fantasy of television." She

---

[10] Malcolm Muggeridge (1977) *Christ and the Media*, Hodder and Stoughton

communicated Christ because of her utter dedication, partially expressed in poverty.

Now there are many other rationalisations that we could make, and we do make from time to time to escape the very real challenge of all this but let me just mention one more that I have often heard.

"It isn't what we have in terms of money and possessions that matter, it's our attitude, it's our lives, not just our money." Now to some extent that is true. Our attitudes are certainly important. Jesus condemned the Pharisee for his self-righteousness, even though he gave tithes of all that he possessed, and it seems that several reasonably wealthy women helped to support Jesus and the Apostles during the three years of their ministry. There is no Christian law about having to give everything away. That's what some of the cults teach but such legalism is absolutely foreign to the teaching of Jesus Christ. And the same was true in the early church where there was tremendous giving and sharing. You remember the story of Ananias and Sapphira, who came under the judgment of God. They were judged by God not because they did not share, but because they lied to the Holy Spirit, and Peter said to them, "Didn't it [the property] belong to you before it was sold? And after it was sold, wasn't the money at your disposal?" (Acts 5:4) In other words it did belong to you, you were free to give it away, you were free not to give it away. There is no legalism, yet having said that, the challenge is still inescapably there. It's not enough to say, "I'll give my heart, I'll give my life to the Lord."

John says in his epistle,

> *If anyone has material possessions and sees a brother or sister in need but has no pity on them, how can the love of God be in that person?*
> 1 John 3:17

John said we ought to lay down our lives for the brethren, and the very least we can do is to lay down our money for them, when they are in need. James says in his epistle,

> *Suppose a brother or a sister is without clothes and daily food. If one of you says to them, "Go in peace; keep warm and well fed," but does nothing about their physical needs, what good is it? In the same way, faith by itself, if it is not accompanied by action, is dead.* James 2:15-17

Jesus said in a very solemn warning about the Judgment Day that one day he would have to say to many people,

> *'Depart from me, you who are cursed, into the eternal fire prepared for the devil and his angels. For I was hungry and you gave me nothing to eat, I was thirsty and you gave me nothing to drink, I was a stranger and you did not invite me in, I needed clothes and you did not clothe me, I was sick and in prison and you did not look after me.'*
>
> *"They also will answer, 'Lord, when did we see you hungry or thirsty or a stranger or needing clothes or sick or in prison, and did not help you?'*
>
> *"He will reply, 'Truly I tell you, whatever you did not do for one of the least of these, you did not do for me.'"* Matthew 25:41-45

The sin of Dives that brought God's awful judgment was the sin of neglect. There is no indication of direct oppression or cruelty. Dives did not order Lazarus to be removed from his gate, he did not kick him as he went by, he did not perhaps even object to Lazarus receiving the leftovers, after his own meal. It wasn't what Dives did that brought God's judgment it was what he did not do. Because he accepted the great chasm between them materially speaking and did nothing about this, it was a great chasm fixed after death only the other way round.

You know there is a kind of deep-rooted feeling that God has so ordered the world that some are poor, and some are rich and that's just the way it is, like some are white and some are black. Most hymn books, thank God, have omitted that appalling verse in a very well-known Victorian hymn, All Things Bright and Beautiful, "The *rich man in his castle, the poor man at his gate. God made them high or lowly and ordered their estate."* That's almost blasphemy. That's the kind of attitude which gave rise to Marxism and the Communist Revolution and was the attitude in Rhodesia and South Africa amongst many white Christians which lead to bloodshed. It was the utterly non-Christian philosophy behind apartheid.

We cannot neglect the appalling needs of hundreds and thousands and millions of people without denying Christ. Because he became poor and laid down his life for us and we are to love as he loved us.

Do you know why Sodom was destroyed? Many people think it was destroyed because of sexual perversion. It's not what the Bible says. In Ezekiel

16:49 *"This was the guilt of your sister Sodom, she and her daughters had pride, surplus of food and prosperous ease, but did not aid the poor and needy."* And that's why the five brothers of Dives were told to listen to Moses and the prophets, because time and time again in the Bible, we have exhortations to care for the poor and warnings about neglecting the needy. God doesn't just want piety, praying and fasting as we saw in Isaiah 58. He wants us to pour out our lives for those who are hungry and homeless, destitute and in need.

Right attitudes are not enough, there must be right actions.

Let me say two things as I close.

First, it is very right that we should challenge one another in love on these lines. Paul urged the Christians at Corinth to excel in the gracious work of generous giving to the poor as they excelled in other spiritual gifts. Recently I have been under tremendous conviction myself. I think God has been teaching me a few lessons over the last few years, but I would suggest that all of us have a very great deal to learn in terms of practical action which is urgently required. At the same time don't be legalistic and don't judge other people. Challenge, yes. Judge, no. And there is a fine but very important difference between those two things.

And the second thing I want to say is try and find your security more and more in the love of God and not in material possessions.

In the body of Christ, we are rich with all the priceless possessions, that are infinitely more valuable than all the material things you could ever possess in this life. Therefore, realise that God loves you, loves you just as you are. He'll never cease to love you and realise that as his grace prompts you in your heart to give more and more generously so you can trust his promise which comes so clearly in his word and that he is able to provide you with blessings in abundance that you may have enough, and give abundantly to every good work.

You and I need to know what it is to be content with enough. Any abundance, any riches above enough, above a very simple lifestyle in today's world. Anything which is in excess of enough must be given away, if we know the love of God in our hearts. Putting it perhaps slightly differently, we must learn to be content with Jesus. Filled with the Spirit of Jesus. We must learn the incredible privilege of being children of the Living God, belonging to him eternally and to one another eternally. We must learn to love one another, support one another. The challenge of all this is going to be considerable. We'll need that love of God flowing strongly amongst us, but as we experience the love of God in this fellowship, as many of us long to do, remember that God's love gives, and gives and gives.

Chapter 2
The Simplicity of Jesus

I heard of a special service that was once planned carefully for laundry workers. The hymns were chosen with a great deal of care and skill. The opening hymn was "O for a Faith that will not shrink" to the tune Lux Benigna. That was followed by "What can wash away my stain" to the tune Eventide and the whole service of course came to a wonderful end with "All things bright and beautiful".

But today, not all things are bright and beautiful in the world that we live, very far from it and wherever we look, whether it's Eastern Europe, the Middle East, Africa or almost anywhere else in the world, things are far from bright and beautiful. In fact, the problems of the world are so vast and complex you can understand why many are depressed, many seem to lack hope altogether and all of us surely need much encouragement.

You see, all is not lost by a long way. Cardinal Suenens put it like this, *"the church has never known a more critical moment in history. From a human point of view there is no hope on the horizons. We do not see from where salvation can come unless from him."*

There is no salvation except in his name and yet at this moment we see in the church the manifestation of the Holy Spirit's action which seems to be like those known to the early church. It is as though the Acts of the Apostles and the letters of St Paul were coming to life again as if God were once more breaking into our history and he added this delightful comment, *"That God, the Spirit of God, can breathe through what is predicted at a human level with a sunshine of surprises."* I love that because the level of faith and expectation by and large even among Christian people is at a pretty low level altogether. We don't expect to see God do mighty things in our midst but even in the gloom, pain, and darkness and though the cloud might hover, God can break through with a sunshine of surprises. As indeed he is doing all over the world as he is revealing again that he is the great and mighty God. A Bishop once said to me that this is the most exciting time in which to be a Christian since the Acts of the Apostles.

And I think that is true, the opportunities are vast, the dangers are vast, everything is at stake and therefore I want to look at Luke Chapter 10 where there you have in the first twenty verses or so, a microcosm of the whole church. We see the mission of the seventy, as the seventy was sent out in the name of Jesus and many take this as a little cameo of what the mission of the church should be like and many Bishops today feel that the church desperately needs to regain a vision of mission and what it's all about. From this passage in Luke 10 I want to share with you what I believe is a seven-fold call to all of us who profess to follow him.

A CALL TO URGENCY

After this the Lord appointed seventy-two others and sent them two by two ahead of him to every town and place where he was about to go. He told them, "The harvest is plentiful, but the workers are few. Ask the Lord of the harvest, therefore, to send out workers into his harvest field. Go!
Luke 10:1-3

Christ's first call to us is come, "Come to me all who are heavy laden and I will give you rest", come everything is now ready. He's always inviting us to come to him. His next call is to go, go on your way, go and preach the gospel, go and make disciples of all nations. Come and then go, that is the movement of the gospel, and today there is no time to lose at all. The harvest is plentiful but the labourers are few and frankly I think much of the church's work and the church's debate and much of the activities of the Christian is like playing bridge on the Titanic after it hit the iceberg. It's just trivia compared with the urgency of the times. We get this note of urgency at the end of Chapter 9, where in verses 59-60, we read,

> He said to another man, "Follow me."
> But he replied, "Lord, first let me go and bury my father."
> Jesus said to him, "Let the dead bury their own dead, but you go and proclaim the kingdom of God."
> Still another said, "I will follow you, Lord; but first let me go back and say goodbye to my family."
> Jesus replied, "No one who puts a hand to the plow and looks back is fit for service in the kingdom of God."

I want you to notice that repetition of the word "first". Lord let me first go and bury my father, let me first say farewell to my family and often we have that sense of priority. Lord first I want to do this, first I must do that, first I've got these plans, first I've got those plans, then yes, then I will consider following you. And Jesus said think first God's kingdom, and there is no time to lose today because I believe time is running out and the end coming fast upon us. Now is the time for the church to wake up and be urgent. If we don't go to the non-believers, they will come to us on their terms and so we see more and more evil in this country, and I sometimes feel we must be absolutely blind and fast asleep not to see the rising tide of evil. The other day a family was rescued from the beach by helicopter because they didn't know the tide was trapping them. And here the tide of evil is trapping us all around and we don't see what God is calling us to do. First, think my Kingdom and get on with it, go we've no time to lose, the harvest now is plentiful and there is a tremendous harvest because not only is time running out, but I also see everywhere a growing spiritual hunger and I find among all kinds of people huge questions about life, God and the future. All these things which of course concerns every single one of us. William Temple said in his days the evangelism of England is a work that cannot be done by the clergy alone, indeed it can't be done by the clergy at all. There can be no widespread evangelisation of England unless the work is undertaken by the people of the church.

Not all are called to be evangelists, but all are called to evangelism and some of us who are clergy spend a great deal of our time in church circles, preaching and encouraging Christians but many of you are in places in your homes and jobs where you are amongst non-Christians all the time. Your circle of friends and acquaintances are unique, and if you're not a witness of Christ right there where God has placed you who else will be. Therefore, we all have a tremendously important role, and it has been estimated, that in spite of all the combined efforts of the churches it is taking one thousand Christians an average of three hundred and sixty-five days to win one person to Christ—that is not good enough. In this country alone ten people are being won to Islam every day, but it is taking a thousand Christians an average of one year to win one person to Christ. You don't have to be a tremendous super Billy Graham but if you were and God blessed your ministry, and you were winning a thousand people to Christ every night of every year it would still take you ten thousand years to win the world for Christ. However, if you as an individual witnessed for Jesus and could help one person find Christ a year and that person helped one other person to find Christ in a year and so on and so on. If we were all doing it, how long would it take us to win the whole world for Christ? Just 32 years. We have a tremendous responsibility to be active where we are, time is running out. The harvest is plentiful, but the labours are few and you mustn't have a thousand labourers working the tiny patch of the harvest to win just one person for Christ a year. We must spread out and to win the world for Christ even one person a year would have an enormous impact if we all did it. After attending a mission meeting a woman wrote to the leader, "Dear *Sir I have come to know Jesus Christ during this mission, and I feel he is calling me to preach the gospel. The trouble is I have twelve children, what can I do?*" He wisely wrote back and said, *"Dear Madam, I am delighted to hear that God has called you to preach the gospel and I am even more delighted he has provided you with a congregation."* So start where you are. It's not just about thinking you will go out to Africa, maybe you will, but start where you are, in your home, in your place of work. Wherever you are, that's where we are to be witnesses for Jesus. And the one thing that is vital is that we do it with all our hearts. John says that to revolutionise the world the only thing needed for us, is for us to live and to spread the gospel of Jesus Christ with real conviction and I think one of the admiring things about Pope John Paul II when he visited the UK, everywhere he went, he took every opportunity to speak not about the church, not about Roman Catholicism but Jesus. And we need to have that same unashamed, unaffected, spontaneous way of talking about Jesus, wherever we go and if we took every opportunity in the supermarkets, markets, in bus queues, anywhere we might be, sharing what Christ means to us there would be a tremendous opportunity for us to share Jesus Christ.

The trouble is that we so often get cluttered up with all kinds of things which are frankly secondary in importance, whether we as individual Christians or the church as an institution. These things that clutter us up may be harmless in themselves, but they prevent us from concentrating on the one thing that is needed. They prevent us from putting first God's Kingdom and stop us from concentrating on the primary task of the church next to worship which is witness of Jesus Christ. We need to learn from our Latin American and African brothers and sisters who all the time will talk about Jesus naturally and spontaneously, but we so often get cluttered up by other things.

It's so easy isn't it to get cluttered up by all kinds of things and eventually we are unable to do what God wants us to do for his Kingdom. And the church sometimes very sadly misses the urgent needs of the day. I often think of the time when the Russian Revolution was raging in Petrograd in 1917. It was just coming to the boil when the Russian Orthodox church, which was in session just a block away from the revolutionary leaders finalising their plans, and the church leaders were having a very heated debate on what colours of vestments the priests should wear. Often today when we are faced with tremendous needs, left, right and centre we can be occupied with trivia and get caught up with ourselves instead of really reaching out with the Gospel of Jesus Christ. A call undoubtedly to urgency, time is running out fast.

A CALL TO UNITY

> *...after this the Lord appointed seventy others and sent them on ahead of Him two by two into every town and place that he was about to come.*
> Luke 10:1

Often in the Acts of the Apostles the disciples went out in pairs or in small groups, their fellowship together was of tremendous importance. They were not to go out on their own except in the most extreme cases, but normally the quality of their fellowship and their relationship together determined the quality of their ministry for Jesus Christ. We are not to be individual disciples; we are part of the body of Christ and every person needs everyone else in the body. I was once in a church in the North of England and listening to someone preach very powerfully about the church being the body of Christ, pointing out that every member of the human body is different, and every part is necessary, and we all need one another, and then the preacher said please turn to the person sitting next to you and say to them "I cannot do without you". Well, I was sitting next to a very attractive young woman I had never met before and I'm afraid I was terribly reserved, and kept my face absolutely set to the front and out of the corner of my eye I noticed to my disappointment that she was doing the same! It is true—we need one another desperately, we cannot do without one another and more and more today we need to be united with one another in love, it is the only way to stand fast against the growing pressures that are around us all the time. You see, if I have a piece of paper I can easily tear it in two with little difficulty. However, if I take two flimsy pieces of paper, put them together with even flimsier pieces of paper, no matter how hard I try I cannot tear them apart. On our own we have no chance of standing against the pressure of the world, the flesh and the devil. The devil's tactics again and again are to divide and to tear Christians apart and then he's won the victory. We need to realise that we have to be more and more together in love. Paul wrote to the Corinthians, after there had been a lot of problems in that church.

> *I urge you, therefore, to reaffirm your love for him. Another reason I wrote you was to see if you would stand the test and be obedient in everything. Anyone you forgive, I also forgive...*
> 2 Corinthians 2:8-10

Why? To keep Satan from gaining the advantage over us. We are not ignorant of his designs. Unless we forgive and remain in active fellowship with one another, he gains the advantage, he splits the church and so comes rushing in like a roaring lion. Those who have gone through very fierce testing in their faith in

Christ have found one of the most important things is for God to bind them together in a community of love.

There is a strong tower which the righteous can run into and be saved, which is the name of the Lord as seen amongst his people and there is a stronghold which we all need when the pressure is on. We all need to hold fast in our relationships with one another. I see today, when the Spirit is doing a tremendous thing in this country, that Satan is trying his utmost to divide Christian from Christian and I see this happening left, right and centre amongst the whole renewal of the Spirit. There is an incredibly fractured Church at the moment. Growing suspicion, fear, hesitation, accusation, pulling apart from one another, that's just what the devil wants us to do. But the Lord sends us out two by two to maintain our fellowship with one another in love, and not just two by two but together as members of one body. And that's the only way in which God is going to bless us, bless our church or bless whatever fellowship it is that we belong to. In the lovely Psalm 133. *"How good and pleasant it is when God's people live together in unity!"* It's like the precious oils, the oil of the spirit, upon the head and running down the beard of Aaron, running on to the collar of his robe. It's like the dew of

Hermon, which pours on the mountains of Zion. For there the Lord has commanded the blessing of life for evermore. It's tremendous when you hold together in love, there the Spirit can work with power, there will be tremendous evidence of abundant life in Jesus. And Jesus himself promised in Matthew chapter 18,

> *...if two of you on earth agree* [The Greek word means 'in symphony'] *about anything they ask for, it will be done for them by my Father in heaven. For where two or three gather in my name, there am I with them.*
> Matthew 18:19-20

God wants us to be united in love. A friend of mine said the effectiveness of our ministry depends upon the fervency of our love for one another. God calls us into a deep unity, not a uniformity but into a deep unity in love. We may be different, and we may have different ideas but we must love and trust one another.

A CALL TO HUMILITY

> *Go! I am sending you out like lambs among wolves.* Luke 10:3

As a little weak lamb in the midst of fierce wolves, how weak and vulnerable a lamb would feel. How weak and vulnerable you and I may feel, in the midst of the most terrific evil that is all around us. I read in a paper in Florida this advertisement.

> "Wanted, person to work on nuclear fissionable isotopes, molecular reactor counters and three phase cyclotonic uranium photosynthesizers—no experience necessary."

We have a task far bigger than that to do and absolutely no experience is necessary. We go out as lambs in the midst of wolves. We have absolutely no strategy as to how we are going to overcome evil apart from the help of God. We have no possible means of bringing one person to Christ apart from the power of the Spirit of God. We have no means of telling people about Jesus apart from the Spirit of God. You and I can do absolutely nothing. Jesus said that without me you can do absolutely nothing and we tend to believe that is a bit of an exaggeration, of course I can do a lot of things but I do need Christ's help from time to time. But the reality is that you and I can do absolutely nothing of spiritual value without the Spirit of God.

God's work must be done in God's way, and with God's power and that power will be marked by a great deal of humble dependent prayer. I think of one of the most impressive churches I have been in the western world. It is an Episcopal church in North America which was packed out with a tremendous mix of culture and age, there were barefooted students in jeans sitting next to company executives in pinstriped suits and all were gloriously mixed up together. There was a most fantastic atmosphere of love and joy and praise. There was form, there was dignity and there was order and yet the Spirit of God was mightily at work in that place. At least at that time, I had never been in a place where there was such a tangible feel of the love of God, you could almost touch it. I've never been so welcomed and so loved. If I had come with anxieties and problems, which I think I did come with, they all vanished because of the atmosphere of love. Surely if God was in any place he was in that church on that morning, and not just that morning, but he was very powerfully there. I also discovered in the coming days that there were plenty of problems, and plenty of weaknesses, there were real tensions within the leadership of the church. The main pastor was not a particularly good preacher and there were other internal problems. The church had God's presence because of four secrets.

The first was prayer, the second was prayer, the third was prayer and the fourth was prayer. They really knew how to pray and God was wonderfully present with tremendous power. It was a very humbling occasion for me because I was asked to preach at the service and I preached briefly. It was a broadcast service every hour on Sunday mornings, and I didn't realise that after the recording ended they went on for another hour and I was expected to preach a second time so I got to my feet a second time and fumbled around with a sermon which I preached very badly and I was trying to get something out and it didn't really come at all and when the rector finished the service he just gave the blessing and someone, for a very short time, sang exquisitely in a tongue and then sang the interpretation. I was told that normally she did not have a very good voice at all. What I found most humbling was that in a very short time she summed up perfectly what I was struggling to say for 20 minutes. God was certainly there but it was in answer to a great deal of believing prayer. It is often said that if we prayed for our leaders as much as we criticise them, we'd have a revival on our hands straight away. I think that there's some truth in that. There was this humility, the disciples knew they were utterly unable to cope with the battle. I send you out as lambs in the midst of wolves yet even though they went into very dangerous territory they saw the power of God at work. No experience necessary but in faith and obedience humbly they went out depending upon the Lord.

A Call to Simplicity

Do not take a purse or bag or sandals; and do not greet anyone on the road. Luke 10:4

Eastern salutations just used to go on and on and on. Jesus said, "Look you've got to stop all this, you've got urgent work to get on with, but especially carry no purse, no bag and no sandals". If we look back to Chapter 9 Jesus was not asking them to do what he was not doing himself.

As they were walking along the road, a man said to him, "I will follow you wherever you go."
Jesus replied, "Foxes have dens and birds have nests, but the Son of Man has no place to lay his head."
Luke 9:57-8

The life of Jesus was clearly marked by simplicity, utter simplicity. He was born into poverty, grew up in a working-class family in a northern town that was not well known or well-liked and people would say "Can any good thing come out of Nazareth?" He had no fixed income and began his work as a preacher. He was utterly dependant on his heavenly Father for meeting his needs. These were sometimes practically met by some of the women who followed amongst the disciples. He had no settled home, He was stripped of his clothes from the cross and buried in a borrowed tomb.

And then we see in 2 Corinthians 8:9:

For you know the grace of our Lord Jesus Christ, that though he was rich, yet for your sake he became poor, so that you through his poverty might become rich.

This was a wonderful mark of the early church; they were willing to share what they had with those who had so little. Look at these two verses, I am going to leave the middle verse out and show verses 32 and 34 of Acts 4, deliberately leaving out verse 33.

All the believers were one in heart and mind. No one claimed that any of their possessions was their own, but they shared everything they had...that there were no needy persons among them. For from time to time those who owned land or houses sold them, brought the money from the sales and put it at the apostles' feet, and it was distributed to anyone who had need.

Here was tremendous sharing of property and possessions for the work of the Kingdom of God. What I have left out is a very important verse. "With great power the apostles continued to testify to the resurrection of the Lord Jesus. And God's grace was so powerfully at work in them all." There was great generosity, great sharing and therefore great power and great grace. They found that where there is great sharing and giving of possessions, there is great grace amongst God's people. You may know the old story about the Pope who one day was showing Thomas Aquinas around the Vatican and the Pope said the church can no longer say "Silver and gold have I none". Aquinas knowing his scripture replied, and neither can it say "in the name of Jesus of Nazareth rise up and walk"

Taking that verse in Acts 3 when Simon Peter said to the lame man at the temple gate called Beautiful. "Silver or gold I do not have, but what I do have I give you. In the name of Jesus Christ of Nazareth, walk." Today we have the treasures, we have the money to a large extent but we do not have power. Today has rightly been called "The generation of the rich fool" We cling to what we have, we want what we cannot have, and we turn a blind eye to those who have nothing. And it's often those who have nothing that are in fact the most generous, and not surprisingly are most blessed by God because they are rich in faith. In that great passage in 2 Corinthians:8 that I previously quoted about the grace of the Lord Jesus. Paul illustrates the giving of a very poor church in Macedonia. He says that you should know about the grace of God there. The abundance of joy and their extreme poverty have overflowed in a wealth of giving on their part, they gave according to their means and beyond their means of their own free will.

One of the most humbling moments in my ministry was receiving a letter one day from a church in Bangladesh. Inside that letter was a cheque for £40 to help us with our work of evangelism in York, and that hurt. Yes, we have given money to Bangladesh and other developing countries but somehow their extreme poverty overflowed in that concern to see people won for Christ in affluent York. A journalist who interviewed Mother Teresa a little time ago, ended her article with these words. "Wherever she goes Mother Teresa leaves behind her a sense of unease. The uncomfortable suspicion that for all her tolerance of us in the West, we have missed the point and are living a ghastly irrelevance." Mother Teresa, without criticising or condemning because she was not that kind of a person, talks about the appalling poverty of the west compared to the Spiritual wealth of places like Kolkata.

Well, it's so easy isn't it to be caught in the rat race, always wanting more and more. The grass always seems to be greener on the other side but someone said it is "because we buy things we do not want to impress people we do not like". Yet so easily we get caught up in the whole rat race and conform to the covetous society in which we live. A modern hero is a poor person who becomes rich rather than a rich person who voluntarily becomes poor, Covetousness we call ambition, hoarding we call prudence, greed we call industry. And so sometimes we worry ourselves sick because of our possessions, and some of the most unhappy people in the world are the wealthiest because they are so worried and anxious about all the possessions which they have.

Richard Foster in *Celebration of Discipline* [11] said:

> *Freedom from anxiety is characterised by three inner attitudes. If what we have we receive as a gift, if what we have is to be cared for by God, if what we have is be available to others, then we will receive freedom from anxiety. This is the inward reality of simplicity.*

And I find that word simplicity very helpful because the Bible has no virtue in poverty. We are not all to become terribly poor just like that. There is nothing special about poverty, it isn't a question about how much you have, it's the inner attitude of simplicity. Proverbs 30:8,9 rightly puts it like this:

> *...give me neither poverty nor riches, but give me only my daily bread. Otherwise, I may have too much and disown you and say, 'Who is the Lord?' Or I may*

---

[11] Richard Foster (2012) *Celebration of Discipline*, Hachette UK

> *become poor and steal, and so dishonor the name of my God.*

We need to learn the level of simplicity and we need to live more simply that some may simply live. Sometimes it is an attitude where we just need to look at the various things that we have got and realise that really they are all belong to God. A woman in our house went around all the rooms in the house and when she went into one room said 'Lord everything in here is yours all those things in my wardrobe are yours, everything in my kitchen is yours, everything is yours, yours, yours, yours. Then she described how she had an inner simplicity to give as she felt the Lord was calling her to give. That was the secret of the generosity of the early church. No-one said that any of the things they possessed were their own. Lord it is all yours and so available for the common good.

Jesus in Luke 12, in the very powerful parable of the rich fool, began like this,

> *Watch out! Be on your guard against all kinds of greed; life does not consist in an abundance of possessions.*

Perhaps this is the number one text for today.

Eventually this person was piling up riches more and more and God said to him,

> *You fool! This very night your life will be demanded from you. Then who will get what you have prepared for yourself?" This is how it will be with whoever stores up things for themselves but is not rich toward God.*

A man who was well known for his tremendous wealth and riches of all kinds, died. He was known to have fabulous things, lots of property and possessions. Someone asked with great curiosity, "How much did he leave" answer—Everything.

A CALL TO SENSITIVITY

> *When you enter a house, first say, 'Peace to this house'...Heal the sick who are there and tell them, 'The kingdom of God has come near to you.'*
> Luke 10:5,9

In other words, be sensitive to the immediate needs of those around you. When Jesus began his ministry his message was crystal clear in Mark 1:15, he said "The time has come...The kingdom of God has come near. Repent and believe the good news!" When Jesus met person after person with all their different needs, he didn't always say repent and believe the gospel. Certainly, that is always the heart of the Christian message.

We need to repent; we need to put our trust in Jesus and when he met with those who were sick he healed them. Those who are hungry he fed them. He met the needs of the individuals when he met them. And there was a tremendous need to be sensitive to the best methods of communications. It's one reason why we try in our missions to take a team with us who try and encourage worship, drama and dance. We live in a visual age, people are increasingly word resistant and they need to experience God's existence or feel God's reality before they will listen to God's word. Through worship we have found that God has been able to speak very powerfully to someone who otherwise would not have heard the gospel at all through words alone. There was a remarkable example of this when I was in a wonderful communion service in Canterbury Cathedral. There were many Bishops and leaders from developing countries. Around 350 Anglican leaders from around the world gathered for an ordinary Anglican communion service. There was a fantastic time of joy and praise and worship. So much so that people from the pubs around Canterbury Cathedral, were coming out of the pubs into the cathedral to find out what the noise was. At the time of the peace when we were invited to greet anyone that we hadn't met before I turned to the person next to me and I said my name is David Watson who are you? From his accent I was unable to place him so asked "where do you come from." He was in fact a tourist from Colorado who had slipped into the cathedral because of the praise and worship. I explained that I was going to be there in a few days time and that his bishop was at the front by the high altar. "Tell me, what do you think of this service. I asked." "I have never been anywhere so alive" "Tell me" I said, "we've only got a moment." "Do you know that the one who makes us alive is Jesus or are you not sure about it" "No "he said "I am not at all sure" "Do you want to know him?" "Yes indeed I do" So we went around the back of the choir of Canterbury Cathedral and as the whole congregation began to sing "Hallelujah, give thanks to the risen Lord" in a tremendous crescendo of praise I had to shout the gospel at him phrase by phrase and he got really quite excited by this and eventually grabbed my hand and said "can we pray?" so I started to pray with him phrase by phrase and he shouted back phrase by phrase and in that way came to the Lord. But what broke through to him was the the joy and praise in a joyless world. That's what cut through and got through to his heart.

Today, the places where you will find that you can more easily share the gospel, are not necessarily in churches, but in your homes with meals or house meetings. That is where people will come to. Why not hold a party for some of your friends or whatever is natural in the particular social environment that you belong to and get someone to speak very briefly there about the Christian faith. I've taken part in hundreds of such meetings in people's homes which are nearly always fruitful. So be sensitive to what is needed as we go out as ambassadors for Jesus Christ.

Whatever house you enter first say peace be to this house, be gracious in your approach. Heal the sick in it. Meet the needs of those who are there. This is a call to sensitivity.

A CALL TO REALITY

Whoever listens to you listens to me; whoever rejects you rejects me; but whoever rejects me rejects him who sent me.
Luke 10:16

In other words, it won't be easy, some will reject you. We need to realise that we are engaged in a tremendous spiritual battle. Alexandra Solzhenitsyn said,

> *But the fight for our planet, physical and spiritual, a fight of cosmic proportions, is not a vague matter of the future; it has already started. The forces of Evil have begun their decisive offensive, you can feel their pressure, and yet your screens and publications are full of prescribed smiles and raised glasses.* [12]

Therefore, today we need trained and disciplined soldiers for Jesus Christ. When I was in the army, you knew a good regiment by the quality of its discipline. Now discipline is not a fashionable word, people don't like to talk about discipline, but if we are called to be disciples of Jesus, discipleship starts with discipline, and without discipleship there is no Christian faith worth speaking of. Bonhoeffer says this about the Christian faith, "Christianity without discipleship is Christianity without Christ." Again and again we see the disciples were called by Jesus to disciplined work

---

[12] Aleksandr Solzhenitsyn, Harvard University address (1978)

and would rebuke them if they were not disciplined in their thoughts and their actions. Paul writing to Timothy as a comparatively young disciple for Christ was told this, "Join with me in suffering, like a good soldier of Christ." [13] No soldier on service gets entangled in civilian disputes since their aim is to please the one who enlists them. Don't get bogged down, don't get entangled, don't get encumbered by secondary matters. We have one aim, to please the Lord who enlists you. There is a tremendous need for such kind of discipline today. In particular we need to know our enemy, who he is, how he works and how to put on the whole armour of God. Be skilled in using spiritual weapons. I wonder if you know what the spiritual weapons are in the battle. The weapon of prayer, the weapon of the word of God which is the sword of the spirit, the weapon of the cross of Jesus Christ, the weapon of the gifts of the Holy Spirit.

These are the weapons we are to use in the spiritual battle. We need to know how to use them. There is no point sending people into battle with all kinds of

---

[13] 2 Timothy 2:3

weapons if they have no idea how to use them. So it is with soldiers of Jesus Christ. Dorothy L. Sayers once said, the average layperson in the church of England is as able to meet an aggressive atheist or agnostic, as a boy with a peashooter can meet a fan-fire of machine guns [14]...and that's sad. This is not an age in which to be soft Christian.

A CALL TO CERTAINTY

The seventy-two returned with joy and said, "Lord, even the demons submit to us in your name."

He replied, "I saw Satan fall like lightning from heaven. I have given you authority to trample on snakes and scorpions and to overcome all the power of the enemy; nothing will harm you. However, do not rejoice that the spirits submit to you, but rejoice that your names are written in heaven."

Luke 10:17-20

Three questions:

Firstly. Is your name written in the book of heaven? When the book of life is opened one day, there will be

---

[14] Dorothy L. Sayers (1995) *Creed or Chaos?* Sophia Inst Press

written all the names of those who put their trust in Jesus Christ as their Lord and Saviour. Will you see your name? Is it there now because you put your trust in Jesus as your Lord and Saviour?

There's a gravestone near where I live in York which reads like this, "Remember friend when passing by, as you are now so once was I, as I am now soon you will be, prepare for death and follow me" and underneath someone has scribbled, "to follow you I am not content until I know which way you went." That is a fair comment because there are only two paths through life; a narrow path leading to life; a broad road leading to destruction, and every one of us is on one of those two paths. We are either on the path leading to life and our names are written in the book of life or we are on that broad road leading to destruction. God in his love puts one obstruction after another, one danger sign, a warning sign to stop us going down that way, he gives us a bible, gives us Christian books, gives us Christian celebrations, gives us churches, above all he gives us the outstretched arms of Jesus on the cross. But if we go past all those warning signs, we only have ourselves to blame for the consequences.

So is your name written in the book of life and are you sure about it?

Secondly. If it is, have you kept your first love for Jesus? Once the risen Christ came to a church in the first century and said I know the fantastic work that you are doing. Jesus commended the church for their hard work, they were sound, they were hard working and they didn't give up. However, he said, "I have this against you—that you've abandoned the love you had at first." Sometimes I confess that I'm challenged by young Christians who have just given their lives to Christ and there is a radiance and a joy and a first love for Jesus that makes mine look rather tarnished and faded and dull. Do we ever feel that we have lost some of our first love of Jesus? Christ said to that church in Ephesus, first repent of your lack of love, if nothing else. Second, do the work you did at first when you came to the cross and were filled with the Holy Spirit. They returned to the scriptures and studied seriously day by day. They burnt their books on the occult and anything that was displeasing to the Lord. That's what it means to do the first work and we need to return to the first love of the Lord.

Thirdly, have you got the assurance that whatever might happen. The Lord reigns?

You see these are very dangerous times, we have great concern about the climate crisis, terrorism, political instability, refugees and humanitarian crises across the world.

We cannot just look to the United States for the solutions. We cannot look to debate in the United Nations. There's only one place we can look and that is up. There may have to be hard work done here on this earth but ultimately our hope is in one direction, in the Lord who reigns. As Gavin Reid a friend of mine once said, "the world will not end with a bang or with a whimper, it will end with a triumphant sound of a trumpet and then all heaven will be let loose." I love that thought of all heaven being let loose, instead of all hell as we often hear. But have you got the confidence that your name is written is in the Book of Life?

Do you still have that first love for Jesus and are you today resting in the fact that even though the future is desperately uncertain, the Lord Reigns and the Lord is fully in control? if so, we must be urgent, united together, going out with the simplicity and the care and the love of Jesus trying to make him known to the world around us.

I hope in our hearts we want to make some kind of response to the Lord, so let's just turn for a moment in prayer to him who is with us now.

Let me ask you this personal question first. Are you quite sure your name is written in the Book of Life? Have you got the absolute assurance that the Lord is your Saviour and Lord? If you are not sure about it, I would invite you, in a very simple prayer, to turn your heart to him and give him your life, receive his spirit into your life.

> *Lord Jesus, thank you that you love me.*
> *I am sorry for all that I have done that is wrong, I need your forgiveness.*
> *I am willing to turn away from all that hurts you.*
> *Thank you for dying on the cross for me and now I give my life to you.*
> *I want you to be my Lord and my Saviour.*
> *Please come into my life, come in now by your Spirit to be with me always.*
> *Thank you Lord Jesus, Amen.*

And then another prayer, if anything that has been mentioned has touched your heart or mind or conscience then use this prayer to give your life afresh to Jesus.

> *Lord, thank you that I know you and you brought me to yourself and for everything that I have experienced of you in the past.*
>
> *Forgive me for losing that simplicity of seeking first your kingdom.*
>
> *Forgive me for losing that first love of you that once I had.*
>
> *Forgive me for getting distracted with other things, however good they are in themselves.*
>
> *Forgive me for coveting what is not mine, that which belongs to another.*
>
> *Wash away all my sins and Lord I give myself afresh to you, I want you to be Lord of my life, Lord of my money and possessions, Lord of my ambitions and my future, Lord of my home and my work. Lord of all.*
>
> *Please fill me with your spirit, that I may live and work to your praise and glory for your holy names' sake. Amen.*

Chapter 3
The Four 'Musts'

An advert in a Sunday newspaper was dominated by the head and shoulders picture of a woman, obviously purring like a cat. The captions above and below read like this: "You self-indulgent, tight-fisted, comfort-lover, you...Don't you really love unashamed luxury? Don't you really hate parting with your hard-earned money? Don't you really love the good things you work for? Don't you really hate being cold or inconvenienced? Why don't you fall in love with the things you really enjoy?"

Now that's the kind of society we have been creating for ourselves in the affluent West — even though we know very well that we are living in a world of extreme hunger and poverty. That kind of advertisement can make you feel a little nauseous. We've previously looked at some of the highly disturbing facts about world poverty and our affluence, and we've seen a lot of hard-hitting principles, without perhaps too many practical suggestions about what to do about them. I've sensed perhaps two reactions coming from a lot of people:

the first group are saying "we're feeling increasingly like a boxer in the ring, wondering where you're going to hit us next". And the second reaction is, "well, please tell us what to do. It's all very well you saying to us, let go of your money, let go of your possessions, and trust the Lord, but please, please be practical about these things. Someone told me a story the other day about a climber who had fallen off a cliff. As he tumbled down a deep gorge, he grabbed hold of the branch of a tree and saved himself. "Help!" he shouted, "is there anyone up there?" A deep majestic voice from the sky echoed through the gorge, "I will help you, my son, but first you must have faith in me." "All right, all right, I trust you." "Then let go of the branch." There was a long pause... "Is there anyone else up there?" Basically, it's a question of coming back to security. Where is our security? Well, instead of just saying "let go" of whatever branch you may be holding on to, here are some practical suggestions for us to think about. I'm not saying I agree with every single one of them, they are not rules we must follow. The gospel of Jesus Christ is that we are not under law, we are under grace. And one constant spiritual danger is that we can so easily slip back into legalism. In some ways we feel more secure if we know exactly what to do and what not to do. Whether we actually do it is a different matter, but at least we know the rules of the game. The cults cash in on this because they present a very hard and fast series of rules on what to do and what not to do. This is one thing that the gospel is quite clear about, that we're no longer under rules and laws. For example, Paul in Galatians 5:1, "It is for freedom that Christ has set us free. Stand firm, then, and do not let yourselves be burdened again by a yoke of slavery." Don't go back into religious rules and regulations, that is not what the Christian faith is all about. Even when Paul wrote to the Corinthian Christians, exhorting them to be more earnest about their giving, he talked about, "...this grace of giving..."[15]

There is no law about giving, no law about a tenth of what you earn or what you have. There's no law about lifestyle. The other reason why I'm a little reluctant to give practical suggestions is that Jesus himself was reluctant about being very specific. Luke 12:13 starts with someone asking Jesus to help him on a financial

---

[15] 2 Corinthians 8:7

problem in his family, "Teacher, tell my brother to divide the inheritance with me." We're having a bit of a family quarrel here and I want you to tell us what is right. Jesus came straight back and said, "Man, who appointed me a judge or an arbiter between you?" I'm not going to enter into this. I'm not going to tell you precisely what to do. Jesus could see that by the very question there was a much more important matter beneath the surface—the man's whole attitude, whole life, whole concern about lifestyle. In verse 15 he goes on to say, "Watch out! Be on your guard against all kinds of greed; life does not consist in an abundance of possessions." In the Jerusalem Bible we read, "...life does not consist in possessions, even when someone has more than he needs." (JB)

In other words, the very desire for rules and regulations on this matter raises the question of where our security really is? That's why Jesus immediately went on to tell the parable of what we call The Rich Fool, a man who put his security in the very uncertain riches of this world. He was storing up for a future of indulgence and excess, when God had to say to him, "You fool! This very night your life will be demanded from you. Then who will get what you have prepared for yourself?"[16] Jesus went on to say to those who were very anxious over this whole area of money, food, clothing, "Therefore I tell you, do not worry about your life, what you will eat; or about your body, what you will wear. For life is more than food, and the body more than clothes."[17] Life is much more than the material things you eat or wear. He went on to say in verse 31 "...seek his kingdom, and these things will be given to you as well." If you are still anxious, if you are still pressing me further, then you are too anxious about these things,

Do not be afraid, little flock, for your Father has been pleased to give you the kingdom. Sell your possessions and give to the poor. Provide purses for yourselves that will not wear out, a treasure in heaven that will never fail, where no thief comes near and no moth destroys. For where your treasure is, there your heart will be also.
Luke 12: 32-34

[16] Luke 12:20
[17] Luke 12:22-23

Frankly our hearts are not right if we cannot realistically face up to the challenge about money and possessions and really do something about them when faced with the needs we have today. However, there is no law about this. Mark the disciple, the writer of the gospel, came from a fairly wealthy family. We know that his mother owned a large house. It became one of the main meeting places for the early church. We know that they had at least one maidservant. When Simon Peter came out of prison he went straight to this house where the church was gathered in prayer. It was quite a well-to-do house. Jesus never indicated it was wrong to live in such a house. Indeed, Jesus himself and the twelve apostles were supported financially by some of the women followers.[18] For men to be supported financially by women in the first century was quite mind-blowing. Jesus did not lay down hard and fast rules about being poor before you could be a wholehearted disciple. Nevertheless, having said all that, may I leave with you four "musts" which I hope won't get musty by our doing nothing about them.

[18] Luke 8:1-3

WE MUST ACCEPT FRUSTRATION OVER GIVING AND SHARING

There are no quick answers to the 2.37 billion people who did not have access to enough safe and nutritious food in 2020.[19] There are no quick answers to the 815 million who are starving at this moment.[20] One danger of a book like this is that we are challenged and then may give what we can afford. However, we then sit back and say, we've done our bit, we've taken action, now what's the next thing we should think about in the Christian faith? I'm afraid it's nothing like as simple as that. That's why the principles are so important to grasp, because the principles, rather than certain practical suggestions, need to go on challenging us at ever increasing depths all the time. Always disturbing, always hurting. I read recently from a missionary in India, a man who has been there for some time and was very much involved in a recent cyclone disaster. He was trying to bring help where he possibly could and said this in an interview.

---

[19] https://www.actionagainsthunger.org.uk/why-hunger/world-hunger-facts
[20] https://www.worldvision.org/hunger-news-stories/global-hunger-facts

"Frustration is an important, sanctifying experience because it removes complacency, that smug feeling that our church is doing plenty for the developing world." There is a terrible injustice in the world which we have to feel as a pain. If we ever lose the frustration, we lose touch with reality in this area. The worst thing is to feel that we have got the subject under control because then it ceases to be in our prayers. We should feel the pain of those people who have no hope, so little joy in life, and feel we are their neighbours. We should be constantly haunted. That I think is a terribly important point, there are no easy answers. That's why it's so wrong to say give a tenth of your money, because that tends to convey the impression that you can keep 9/10 to yourself. As an example, John Wesley worked out what was enough for him and stayed with that amount, so as his income increased his giving increased. The point being that we should never cease to be challenged, never cease to be disturbed, never cease to be haunted and frustrated by the immense poverty and injustice of the world in which we live.

WE MUST AIM AT LIFE AND NOT JUST AT GENEROUS CHARITY

Again, so much of the passage we're looking at in Luke 12 is about life. Verse 15 again "Watch out! Be on your guard against all kinds of greed; life does not consist in an abundance of possessions." It's our life, our attitudes to our life and other people's lives, it's our lives reflected in our lifestyles that are all important. We must increasingly live as Jesus lived if we are to have any credibility in today's unjust world. How did Jesus and the disciples live? How did Jesus and the apostles live? They had a common purse. One man looked after the common fund, and he would give out of it to the poor if Jesus directed that. They shared their resources together. They became a real, caring community. Their common purse symbolised their serious commitment to one another as well as to the master. In Acts it was very similar, no-one said that any of the things they possessed were their own. They had everything in common. When there was a need they shared what they had with those who had not. When a Pentecostal church over in Corinth heard about a high church in Jerusalem which was going through a time of famine, they immediately sent relief. They shared regardless of differences of traditions and style of worship. The Apostle Luke writing in Acts also makes it clear, that they did not abolish private property or private possessions. There was no law about that. But the Greek tense makes it clear that they often sold their possessions, not just on one occasion. However, when a need arose, they found something they could sell or something they could use to help somebody else, they did it often. It was part of their lifestyle wherever the need arose. In other words, they made their resources, they made their money, their possessions, their property unconditionally available to one another. That's what their commitment to Christ and to his body meant in practical terms and it was very powerful. No wonder we read again and again that the word of God increased, and the number of disciples multiplied. More followers were added to the faith. It didn't stop with the New Testament either. In 125AD a Christian philosopher describes the economic sharing of a church in the 2nd Century,

> *They love one another. He that hath, distributeth liberally to him that has not. If they see a stranger they bring him under their roof and rejoice over him as if it were their own brother. If they hear that any of their own number is imprisoned or oppressed for*

the name of their Messiah, all of them provide for his needs. And if there is among them a man that is poor and needy and they have not an abundance of necessaries, they fast two or three days that they may supply the needy with their necessary food." [21]

We've asked for practical suggestions, well there they are. By 250AD the church in Rome alone supported 1500 needy people. No wonder the world of that day experienced the life and love of the risen Lord Jesus. Here was Christ on earth, the same Lord Jesus in his body, by his spirit, who walked this earth in poverty and gave himself and everything for those in need. No wonder the world of that day, the mighty Roman Empire, was conquered by such a quality of love, for the body of Christ was truly at work. You see, the only unique thing that you and I have to offer to the world is the life and love of Jesus Christ. Anyone can preach sermons or organise services or sing songs, if they happen to have those gifts. But when we start living as Jesus lived and become in reality and with integrity

---

[21] Aristides "The Just" quoted in *A New Eusebius: Documents Illustrating the History of the Church to A.D. 337* (SPCK Church History), Second Edition, James Stevenson, 28 May 1987

the body of Christ filled with the spirit of love, then that is powerful and real in the world of today. The only unique thing we have to offer is the life of Jesus, not just the words about him. Life which comes in that deep, costly, sharing, sacrificial, laying-down-your-life love.

WE MUST GO ON WORKING ON THIS THEME

The man who didn't sort out the place of possessions in his life was called by Jesus a fool. He never really worked it through. He probably knew about the challenge, he knew about the needy, I'm sure, but he never worked it through, and God said to him, fool! At death he had nothing. "You fool! This very night your life will be demanded from you. Then who will get what you have prepared for yourself? This is how it will be with whoever stores up things for themselves but is not rich toward God."

I hope this series will just be a starter for many of us with a lot of hard thinking and sacrificial giving to do in the future. According to Ron Sider's book,[22] we need to change at three levels. First, our personal lifestyle, showing that we are willing to change and showing a real concern for the poor as individuals. Second, our corporate lifestyle as a church, so that moving and working together we can help one another. It is difficult and threatening so that by working together we have another model to show the covetous society in which we live. When people talk about standards of living, it has nothing to do with life. It means standards of getting, standards of possessing. Standard of living is a total misnomer. We could have a standard of living, a quality-of-life which all the gadgets and luxuries in the world will never produce. That's living. And the third thing, which is extremely difficult to do is to change the structures of the society in which we live.

ITV planned 3 programmes on successive Wednesdays showing something of the oppression of blacks in South Africa. I was appalled to see that the powerful company Tate & Lyle managed to stop the

---

[22] *Rich Christians in an Age of Hunger: Moving from Affluence to Generosity*, 2015, Thomas Nelson

showing of one of those episodes. They also took out a court case against the producer of the films.[23] In the discussion that came when the episode eventually was shown, I thought the producer showed enormous integrity. I took the liberty of writing to encourage him and say that I admired him for his courage and integrity. He replied saying that he had received hundreds of letters from people along the same lines.

We should not allow big powerful companies to silence the voice of people exposing the injustices of today. We can't do much about it but we need to think what we can do. I want you also to notice the Bishop of Winchester's recent comment on this subject, "let us never forget the ruthlessness of those principalities and powers against which we fight." It's never going to be easy.

---

[23] Working for Britain, the 3rd in a series The South Africa Experience by producer Antony Thomas, December 1977, Associated Television.
https://www.nytimes.com/1977/12/20/archives/british-judge-approves-showing-of-tv-program-about-south-africa.html

In Acts 20 Paul talks with the Ephesian elders and in a magnificent passage spells out the great power of Christian ministry. His closing words to them are these,

> *In everything I did, I showed you that by this kind of hard work we must help the weak, remembering the words the Lord Jesus himself said: "It is more blessed to give than to receive."*
> Acts 20:35

They knelt down on the shore, they prayed, they embraced one another, they wept. Because they knew they would never see each other again this side of heaven. Those were his last words, "It is more blessed to give than to receive".

WE MUST TAKE SOME ACTION

Even though it might be for most of us only one step at a time. I find preaching and teaching this subject very disturbing for me personally and have had to take some action myself. I can't just preach and do nothing.

Let me close with these words from Ron Sider, "I am convinced that simple living is a biblical imperative for Christians in affluent lands." It's a must. We are not committed to a simple lifestyle. We only have one absolute loyalty and that is to Jesus and his kingdom. But the head of this kingdom is the God of the poor, and hundreds of millions of his poor are starving. By all means avoid legalism and self-righteousness but have the courage to commit yourself to some specific method for moving towards a just, personal lifestyle. Will we dare, to measure our living standards by the needs of the poor rather than by the lifestyles of our neighbours? "Where your treasure is, there will your heart be also."

Chapter 4
You Cannot Lose

But love your enemies, do good to them, and lend to them without expecting to get anything back. Then your reward will be great, and you will be children of the Most High, because he is kind to the ungrateful and wicked.
Luke 6:35

GOD IS ON THE SIDE OF THE POOR

Jesus is speaking, picking out some words from that verse. "Lend...without expecting to get anything back. Then...you will be children of the Most High, because he is kind to the ungrateful and wicked." And it's just as well that God is so kind to the ungrateful and to the wicked, otherwise none of us would experience much of the kindness of the Lord, only his judgement, which we deserve. Here is one glorious truth which emerges so clearly from the Scriptures, that God is impartial, he is no respecter of persons. He is rich to all who call upon him, he sends rain and sunshine, snow and ice on the just and on the unjust. But although God is impartial, although God loves every single person no matter what their heart is like, no matter what their life is like, no matter what their bank balance is like, no matter how rich you are compared to those who have nothing, the first vital truth I want to stress is that God is always on the side of the poor. Simply because he is equally concerned with the wellbeing of us all, he has to be on the side of the poor because hardly anybody else is. Most of us, even in church, oppress the poor and crush the needy. If that is a chilly remark to make, may I say that we do this not because we are deliberately cruel, we would be horrified at the very suggestion. But so often by our affluent lifestyle and our sheer neglect, we are inevitably adding to the suffering of others almost certainly without realising it.

People in rich countries consume up to 10 times more natural resources than those in the poorest countries.[24] Do we care? We know these facts or can very easily find out these facts if we take the trouble to, so what are we who are rich—very rich compared with so many—what are we really doing about it? Is it any wonder that in the bible God often opposed the

---

[24] https://friendsoftheearth.uk/sites/default/files/downloads/overconsumption.pdf

rich? Sometimes in no uncertain terms. Amos, who was a shepherd, never minced his words when he spoke to those who were rich. He said to the wealthy women of Mount Samaria, "Hear this word, you cows of Bashan...bring us some drinks!"[25] They were probably crushing the needy by their lifestyle and by their neglect, not necessarily by deliberate acts of injustice. Is it any wonder that in the bible God frequently showed himself to be on the side of the poor?

> *He defends the cause of the fatherless and the widow, and loves the foreigner residing among you, giving them food and clothing.*
> Deuteronomy 10:18

> *Religion that God our Father accepts as pure and faultless is this: to look after orphans and widows in their distress...*
> James 1:27

> *Listen, my dear brothers and sisters: Has not God chosen those who are poor in the eyes of the*

---

[25] Amos 4:1

> *world to be rich in faith and to inherit the kingdom he promised those who love him? But you have dishonored the poor.*
> James 2:5-6

God is a God of justice and if there is to be any justice in this world, God must be on the side of the poor. Otherwise, he would simply be encouraging the rampant injustice of today's world when there is an increasing gap between those who have and those who have not.

GOD IDENTIFIES WITH THE POOR

So much so that Proverbs 19:17 says, "Whoever is kind to the poor lends to the Lord." If Jesus were here in the flesh today and you went outside and found him poor, in rags, cold, hungry, with no money, would you help him? Of course you would. You wouldn't hesitate. "Whoever is kind to the poor lends to the Lord." Jesus himself said the same thing very clearly in the parable we know so well,

> *Come, you who are blessed by my Father; take your inheritance, the kingdom prepared for you since the creation of the world. For I was hungry and you gave me something to eat, I was thirsty*

> *and you gave me something to drink, I was a stranger and you invited me in, I needed clothes and you clothed me, I was sick and you looked after me, I was in prison and you came to visit me.'*
>
> And they all said, *"Lord, when did we...?"* Answer: *"...whatever you did for one of the least of these brothers and sisters of mine, you did for me."*
>
> Matthew 25: 35-40

"Jesus is hungry in the hunger of men. Jesus is ruthless with the stranded pavement dweller. Jesus is shivering with the shivering victim of the cyclone. Jesus is ravaged in the ravaged and damaged crops. Jesus is cold in the cold lifeless bodies."[26]

Richard Wurmbrand, when in years of solitary confinement suffered greatly for his faith in Jesus Christ.[27] The only people he met in 3 years were those who tortured him. He longed that the Lord should say

---

[26] Source unknown
[27] Wurmbrand: *Tortured for Christ - The Complete Story* 1 April 2018 by The Voice of the Martyrs, David C Cook Publications

something to him and as he listened he heard this, "Aaaaaagh!" It was a cry of anguish from someone being tortured down the corridor for his faith in Christ. He realised that the Lord was suffering through the suffering of the members of his body. In all our affliction, he himself is afflicted. That's how God spoke.

Supremely, we see God's identification with the poor and needy in the person of his own son when he was on earth—born in a cattle shed, son of a working-class home, in a despised area "Nazareth! Can anything good come from there?"[28] His parents were too poor to bring an ordinary offering to the temple for the purification. The ordinary offering was a lamb. The very poorest people brought just two pigeons, which Jesus's family brought.[29] He was a refugee baby in Egypt. He was an immigrant in Galilee. As an itinerant preacher he had no income, no home, no spare clothes, sometimes no food at all. "...though he was rich, yet for your sake he became poor..."[30] His

---

[28] John 1:46
[29] Luke 2:24
[30] 2 Corinthians 8:9

ministry could be accurately summed up in his own words,

> *The Spirit of the Lord is on me, because he has anointed me to proclaim good news to the poor. He has sent me to proclaim freedom for the prisoners and recovery of sight for the blind, to set the oppressed free.*
> Luke 4:18

Jesus assured John the Baptist that he was the Messiah because of his care for the poor and the needy. That was part of the evidence and the mark of his Messiahship. Incidentally, he sent his disciples out into exactly the same sort of ministry, instructing them to adopt exactly the same lifestyle. Why? Because God has always identified himself with the poor. On the cross, Jesus had absolutely nothing, he was penniless, helpless, humiliated, mocked, and naked. His body was placed in a borrowed grave. Yet Paul repeatedly refers to the power of the cross, and the cross has always had tremendous power to change people's lives, to break the very bondage of Satan. Why is there so much power in the cross of Jesus Christ? Why has all power been given to Jesus? Why is his name above every name that has been named? It is because he was willing to lay on one side his riches and glory. He was willing to become our servant. He was willing to become poor for our sake, willing to go to death on a cross that we might live, bearing our sin. God supremely identifies with the poor in Jesus Christ. In the bible one of the marks of false teachers is a preoccupation with money. They become financially well-off because of claiming to do the Lord's work. I don't believe there is any great virtue in extremes of poverty, of course not. But if you and I are to be the body of Christ with some credibility for today's world, we must increasingly live as Jesus lived. We must increasingly identify ourselves with the poor and adopt Jesus' lifestyle, most of us have a long, long way to go in this respect. A journalist, having interviewed Mother Teresa of Calcutta, ended an article with these words, "Where she goes, Mother Teresa leaves behind her a sense of unease, the uncomfortable suspicion that for all her tolerance towards us in the West, we have missed the point and are living a ghastly irrelevance." I wonder if you sometimes feel that when you have bought something you haven't really needed? Afterwards you maybe feel ashamed or guilty, as though the whole thing was a ghastly irrelevance. Ron Sider in his book, *Rich*

Christians in an Age of Hunger, puts it more forcefully, "If we fail to feed the needy, we do not have God's love, no matter what we say. Regardless of what we do or say on a Sunday, affluent people who neglect the poor are not the people of God."[31]

GOD WORKS THROUGH THE POOR

Most of the great men and women of God and most of the prophets and apostles, were poor, uneducated people. Most of them would never have fulfilled the academic requirement for the Anglican ministry today – and probably just as well. Spurgeon once said to his students who were training to be preachers, 'Remember to keep the message simple, and don't preach over people's heads. Our Lord said, "feed my sheep", not "feed my giraffes."'[32] Over the years many of the preachers and prophets God has used have been ordinary people and some of them poor. There have been notable exceptions of course, but look at Joseph the slave, or Amos the shepherd, or Peter,

---

[31] *Rich Christians in an Age of Hunger: Moving from Affluence to Generosity*, 2015, Thomas Nelson
[32] Charles Spurgeon, *Feed My Sheep* Sermon #3211, p. 6. As cited http://www.spurgeongems.org/vols55-57/chs3211.pdf

James and John all fishermen. Ordinary working folk. Folk who heard Jesus gladly, folk who followed Jesus, folk who turned the first-century world upside down. Yes, there was Doctor Luke and the scholar Paul who were exceptions. But Paul himself said there weren't many mighty; noble; rich or powerful people that God chose. Instead, God chose ordinary folk so that no one could boast in his presence. Look at Peter and John at the Gate Beautiful with the lame man[33]. The man was asking for money and most of us would probably have said, perhaps a little bit ashamed, "well alright here's 50p or a pound", or even a fiver if we were feeling very generous. But Peter had to say this "Silver or gold I do not have." We haven't got anything, but we'll give you what we've got. "In the name of Jesus Christ of Nazareth, walk." And he leapt up and walked. And why did they have nothing? It was because a few verses earlier they were sharing all that they had, little though it was, with those in need.[34] That's why they had nothing. But they had the power of God with them. Sometimes we have so much that we see little of

---

[33] Acts 3:1-9
[34] Acts 2:45

God's power at work. A few centuries ago, a rotund cardinal watched wagonloads of gold and silver coming into the Vatican to fill the papal treasury. 'Holy Father', he said to the Pope, 'the Church can no longer say, silver and gold have I none.' And the Pope looked very sad, remembering the second half of that verse. 'Neither can the Church say, "in the name of Jesus Christ of Nazareth rise up and walk."'[35]

It's often the poor who are rich in faith. In 1840 some American Baptists went to the east coast of India to start working among the affluent and influential upper class. They slaved away for 25 years and produced less than a hundred converts. A little time after that, a man and his wife were convinced that what St Paul said was true, that God often took what was weak and foolish and despised, and they were the people that God used. They went to a group of people called the 'untouchables', who were very poor. They

---

[35] According to Cornelius à Lapide, Thomas Aquinas once called on Pope Innocent II whilst he was counting out large amounts of money. Cited by F. F. Bruce, *The Book of Acts*, Revised Edition (Grand Rapids: William B. Eerdmans Publishing Company, 1988), pp. 77-78.

were warned by the older missionaries that they were wasting their time but in just four years hundreds of these 'untouchables' were won to Jesus Christ, including many who became fine Christian workers. John Wesley once said that "everywhere we find the labouring part of mankind are the readiest to receive the gospel."[36] Wesley himself was willing to live very simply indeed, giving away most of what he had. Today the church in the West has largely failed in industrial areas because we have concentrated too much on the rich, influential, powerful and intellectual. Is that one reason why we have increasingly neglected the Developing World? And is that one reason why God has withdrawn so much of his life and power from us? The really poor churches in South America or Eastern Europe or Korea are throbbing with spiritual life compared to most of us. Sometimes crude, simple, noisy, fervent, but absolutely alive. When Richard Wurmbrand was in a communist prison for his faith, he was at one time

---

[36] John Wesley 1771, quoted in Howard A. Snyder, 2005, *Radical Renewal: The Problem of Wineskins Today*, Wipf and Stock Publishers

with a hundred other prisoners in a cell. The conditions were indescribable. The food allowance was one slice of bread per week. Yet in spite of this the Christian prisoners nearly all tithed their slice of bread. Some gave one slice every ten weeks, some gave one slice every four weeks or three weeks, whatever they chose to do. What for? First of all to worship God and to sacrifice to him. But in practical terms it was given to those who were sick in that cell. Or the tithed bread was given to some of the non-Christians as an expression of God's love for them. Sometimes it was set aside so that they might have regular services of Holy Communion. When Christians were really troubled by hunger, how did they find victory? By fasting. Wurmbrand said that when they voluntarily gave up what was their right, even though it was one slice a week, they found that they had victory over hunger. Is it any wonder that they experienced, to quote Wurmbrand, "a beauty in Christ they had never known before"?[37] Is it surprising that God was manifestly with them with great power? An extreme case of course, but when we love one another

---

[37] Richard Wurmbrand: *Tortured for Christ*, op.cit.

or begin to do so as Christ has loved us, God is in our midst. God frequently works through those who are poor.

GOD WANTS US TO CONCENTRATE MORE ON THE POOR

By and large we are not very thankful, we are not very generous, we are not very radiant. Perhaps it is because we have too much and are bound by an evil spirit of covetousness. When Paul was urging Christians in Corinth to give more generously, he spoke about the church in Macedonia. During a time of affliction the joy of the church there had overflowed in a wealth of liberality. They were really afflicted, they were desperately poor, yet they were filled with joy and overflowed in generosity. Now, Paul said to those in Corinth, you have excelled in so many spiritual gifts, excel in this gracious gift as well. He goes on to say in the next chapter, 2 Corinthians:9, that God loves a cheerful giver. The word cheerful in Greek really means a 'hilarious giver', someone who can't get rid of their bank notes quick enough, out of joy for the Lord. No doubt we are threatened by these things, hence the vital need to become a real, caring community, sharing together for Jesus Christ. For some of us it may mean sharing together literally in our homes and extended families. Certainly you can release more money in that way. I've been in such a situation for five years now and I know that you can live a little bit more simply, you can give more away by sharing like that. Even if the Lord does not call us to live like that, we need to share together in fellowship much more, we need to let money flow much more freely amongst us. Paul says:

> *At the present time your plenty will supply what they need, so that in turn their plenty will supply what you need. The goal is equality*
> 2 Corinthians 8:14

In other words if you've got some and they haven't, give to them. Later on, when they've got some and you haven't got it, they'll give back to you. Share together freely. That's the kind of principle Paul is talking about. That's why we need to strengthen our love for one another, so that when we are feeling challenged or threatened, our security is really in the love of God. A love that is tangibly expressed through members of his family. Then we are much freer to give and give and give, instead of get and get and get, which is the policy of the world. Ron Sider again, "the church should consist of communities of loving defiance."[38] I love that and I believe that in a gentle, loving, gracious, humble way we need to challenge the greed and covetousness of today's world. "But" said Ron Sider, "instead, I'm afraid, so often the churches consist largely of comfortable clubs of conformity." Which are we? Don't let the world around you squeeze you into its own mould, says Paul. A very mouldy mould, I can assure you. Now on our own, I think we are all helpless with all the pressures around us. But if we become that real, loving, caring community of loving defiance, agreeing together to adopt a simpler lifestyle, agreeing together to give more to the poor, agreeing together to share more freely with one another, we really will begin to live as Jesus lived. As one Hindu said to a Christian leader in India, "On that day when we see Jesus Christ living out his life in you, then we will flock to your Christ."

---

[38] Ron Sider, *Rich Christians in an Age of Hunger* (London: Hodder and Stoughton, 1990) p. 200

GOD IS NO ONE'S DEBTOR

Although Jesus tells us in Luke 6 to give or to lend expecting nothing in return, he goes on to say that our reward will be great.

> *Give, and it will be given to you. A good measure, pressed down, shaken together and running over, will be poured into your lap. For with the measure you use, it will be measured to you.*
> Luke 6:38

God wants to pour back so much when we give to him. One rich farmer was known to be extraordinarily generous and yet he seemed to get richer and richer. Someone asked him how it was possible and he answered like this, "Well I keep shovelling it in God's bin, and God keeps shovelling it in my bin. And God's got the bigger shovel." If you're a shrewd businessperson and think you're onto a good thing here, let me say that we are to give, says Jesus, expecting nothing in return. And if we do that, out of love for the Lord and concern for those in need, countless Christians have proved time and time again that God is no one's debtor. In various ways he will load you with benefits. Paul once wrote that when the rest of the apostles gave their blessing on his ministry to the gentiles, they laid out one urgent condition, "that we should continue to remember the poor". "The very thing," he added, "I had been eager to do all along."[39] I hope that will be true of each one of us as God leads us into different kinds of ministry. That we will remember that God is concerned about those who are poor in his world.

---

[39] Galatians 2:10

Chapter 5
Simple Living

At Christmas I was given, by my wife, a poster which more or less sums up the attitude of us in the affluent West — "My tastes are simple; I like to have the best." We may say, "yes I've got quite simple tastes." However, the best that we often seek is not the kind of best that God longs for us to have. He's got something much richer in store for us. As a church we have much still to learn about sacrificial giving. I know of many other churches that take giving much more seriously than we do. I read from a missionary from Wycliffe Bible Translators, "The church we attended last Sunday was the United Native African Church. The offering took 35 minutes and the sermon 13! The offering was taken by the church clerk, calling out each name, each person responding verbally with an amount they would give. Then an usher would go to collect the offering, giving change as necessary."

In Luke chapter 21, we read the very familiar story of the poor widow and her mite. It highlights some of the most important principles behind Christian giving. But there's one very interesting point which might be easily missed. It comes in the first 4 verses of Luke 21. Mark begins his version of that incident with these words, "Jesus sat down..."[40] and Luke begins "As Jesus looked up..."[41] From the context, it seems to be quite clear that Jesus was sitting in the temple, utterly exhausted and, like many of us when we're utterly exhausted, probably had his head in his hands and was just as weary as can be. If you look at the context, by glancing at one or two verses in the preceding chapters, you will see why he was so exhausted, and no doubt depressed and maybe very weary indeed with the men and women he'd come to save. In chapter 19 verse 41, *"As he approached Jerusalem and saw the city, he wept over it."* In verse 45, he entered the temple and began to drive out those who sold, saying to them, *"It is written,"* he said to them, *"'My house will be a house of prayer'; but you have made it 'a den of robbers.'"*. The next verse, *"Every day he was teaching at the temple. But the chief priests, the teachers of the law and the leaders among the people were trying to kill him."* And then in chapter 20 verse 2

---

[40] Mark 12:41
[41] Luke 21:1

they come to him and say, *"Tell us by what authority you are doing these things," they said. "Who gave you this authority?"* trying to trick him again and again. Verses 19-20 *"The teachers of the law and the chief priests looked for a way to arrest him immediately, because they knew he had spoken this parable against them. But they were afraid of the people. Keeping a close watch on him, they sent spies, who pretended to be sincere. They hoped to catch Jesus in something he said, so that they might hand him over to the power and authority of the governor".* In verse 27 the Sadducees came with an argument to him. In these preceding chapters you see one thing after another from those who wouldn't believe; are trying to trap him; trying to oppose him; or who are trying to hound him to death. After that long weary episode Jesus just sat down in the temple and put his head between his hands. Perhaps he wept again. He was certainly exhausted. He still had all the suffering and agony of the cross to go through in the immediate future. Yet what he saw in this one poor needy widow as he looked up, I believe really refreshed him, even though humanly speaking what she did was almost nothing. That point alone really encourages me and I hope it encourages you. I'm sure that as Jesus looks upon his church today, let alone the world, at times he is very, very sad. His spirit is constantly grieved. Putting it in human terms, I'm sure he must put his head in his hands again and again and weep over us for all our quarrelling, bickering, jealousy, infighting, arguing, debating and talking, when the world is starving for the love of God. I am sure we sadden him time and time again. You may feel that you have virtually nothing to give, little or no money; no gifts worth offering to the church; you are not gifted in music, singing, dance or drama. You may feel you have nothing to give at all. However, I believe that every single one of us without exception can still refresh and delight the heart of Jesus. If you know him and love him at all, I'm sure you long to do just that, to bring him real pleasure, real delight in a sad world and a tragically dead or dying church. Well you can refresh him and fill him with joy, whoever you are, whatever you do, if we learn some of the lessons from this poor, widow.

I would like to draw out three points about her gift.

IT WAS A GIFT OF LOVE

In Mark's version of the story we read this,

> *Jesus sat down opposite the place where the offerings were put and watched the crowd putting their money into the temple treasury. Many rich people threw in large amounts. But a poor widow came and put in two very small copper coins, worth only a few pence.*
> Mark 12:41-42

They were incredibly small coins. Take a look at a 1p coin, it's so small and insignificant. This was the smallest coin that they had in those days, just as the 1p is the smallest coin we have and use today.[42] But

---

[42] They are widely believed to be what are known as lepton (which means "small" or "thin') coins minted by Alexander Jannaeus, King of Judea from 103 to 76 BCE and the great grandnephew of King Judah Maccabee. Two lepta were worth a quadrans, the smallest Roman coin, and a lepton was the least valuable coin that circulated in Judea.
The term "mite", which is used today, did not exist at the time the coins circulated. They only became known as mites many centuries later. "Mite" as used here means "small cut piece" in Old Dutch and only came into use in the 14th century in Flanders. It is also used in the King James Bible, which brought

notice, she didn't just put in one, she put in two. Although with a perfectly good conscience she could, out of her poverty, just have put in the one coin. But the mere fact she chose to put in both those small coins shows that what she offered to God was a gift of love, a beautiful sacrificial gift of love. Rather like another occasion when Jesus was in Bethany at the house of Simon the Leper, and a woman came with an alabaster box of ointment, of pure nard, very costly we're told by Mark. And she broke the flask and poured it over his head. And they were all indignant, *"'Why this waste of perfume? It could have been sold for more than a year's wages and the money given to the poor.' And they rebuked her harshly."*[43] But Jesus says two things in reply to the critics, one, she has done a beautiful thing to me. It thrilled Jesus because here was such an obvious expression of sheer love, just like this poor widow who put in two mites. Sheer love. John says about a similar incident when a woman

---

the term and the Widow Mite's story to many millions of people beginning in 1611.
Source: https://coinweek.com/ancient-coins/what-are-widows-mite-coins/
[43] Mark 14:4-5

broke an alabaster box of ointment in another house in Bethany, the house was filled with the fragrance of the ointment. Very beautiful, but what was even more beautiful, I believe, the house was filled with love, the fragrance of love for Jesus. And there's nothing more beautiful than that. You see, it's not what we give that counts, but how we give and why we give it. God looks upon our hearts. The rich men gave out of a sense of religious duty perhaps. But the widow in the temple and the woman in the house at Bethany gave out of sheer love. And that more than anything was really beautiful in the eyes of Jesus, it deeply moved him. *"...she has done a beautiful thing to me."*[44]

The second thing that Jesus said about this woman in the house at Bethany, *"She has done what she could"*[45]. Others had done very much more, materially speaking, but both this woman in the house in Bethany and the widow in the temple, they had done what they possibly could have done. Simply out of love for God or for Jesus Christ. Two rich Christians from the West visited South Korea not so long ago.

[44] Mark 14:6
[45] Mark 14:8

They saw a young child harnessed to a plough and the plough led by an old man. Later they asked about this and the villagers explained that a church was being built in the village and the family had no money to contribute, so they sold the only ox they had and gave the money to build the church. That's why the young lad was pulling the plough. As Christians we can learn from that story some of the secret of sacrificial giving and real love for Jesus. One of the most humbling experiences I remember was when I received a letter from a church in Bangladesh. Inside the letter was a cheque for £40 to help us here in York with our evangelism. From poverty-stricken Bangladesh. Came a beautiful offering to Jesus, to help us in our affluence spread the good news about him. I found it a very, very difficult thing to receive. Paul wrote to the Christians at Philippi who had been very generous to him, that he did not really need the money. He said, *"I have received full payment and have more than enough. I am amply supplied, now that I have received from Epaphroditus the gifts you sent. They are a fragrant offering, an acceptable sacrifice, pleasing to God."* [46]

---

[46] Philippians 4:18

The thing that pleased God, the thing that was thrilling to Paul, was that their gifts were so obviously out of sheer love for Jesus and for their brother.

IT WAS A GIFT OF FAITH

In chapter 21 of Luke's gospel verse 4, *"All these people gave their gifts out of their wealth; but she out of her poverty put in all she had to live on."* Now the rich, as Mark tells us, put in plenty of money into the treasury. But they could well afford to do so and it really made no difference to their way of life. For them it was no sacrifice; they still had all their comforts, all the luxuries they wanted because they had an abundance of possessions, they gave out of their abundance what they could easily afford and they hardly noticed it, if at all. Not so with the woman. A man was singing in church one day and it was one of his favourite hymns, he was singing it with all his heart, *"Were the whole realm of nature mine, that were an offering far too small...my all"*.[47] As he was singing, his hand was in his pocket groping for the offering

---

[47] *When I Survey the Wondrous Cross,* Isaac Watts 1674-1748, Public Domain

which he was having to put into the bag which was coming round. And he was feeling very carefully to ensure it was a £1 coin and not a £2 coin by some ghastly mistake. *"Love so amazing, so divine."* £1 is sufficient as a response. We mustn't get fanatical about these things. A fanatic is someone who loves Jesus more than you do.

But this woman put in all that she had. Widows were notoriously poor in those days; they couldn't have any job at all. They lived a hand to mouth existence, hoping every day for just enough to eat by which to survive. And therefore, by giving to God all that she had, she really pushed herself into a position where she really had to trust the Lord for her very life. *"Give us this day our daily bread".* Now I doubt that many of us have had to pray that part of the Lord's prayer with real urgency; *"Give us this day our daily bread".* I doubt if many of us have come to a place where we have had to depend upon him for our daily existence like that. For this woman, once she had given all that she had, she then had nothing. It was a gift of faith. She was now totally and utterly dependent on the Lord for her very life. In a less dramatic way perhaps but very moving, I heard a lovely story from a missionary setting up a worshipping community in Israel, who urgently needed $5000 to rent a property for their little community. They had to put down two years rent in advance. A Christian fellowship in the US urgently needed $10,000 for their work. And one day $5000 arrived for their work and they were thrilled, and they praised the Lord. But as they went on praying, the Lord told them to give the whole amount to the community in Israel. That was a test of faith, but they obeyed. They sent the whole amount which supplied the needs of the community in Israel, and then they received another cheque, within a week, this time for $11,000, more than their total need. This kind of story can be repeated hundreds and thousands of times over. God is no person's debtor. In the context of Paul receiving the fragrant offering from the Philippian Christians, he reminded them that *"...my God will meet all your needs according to the riches of his glory in Christ Jesus."*[48] Yes, what you sent me was lovely and beautiful and God will honour you in that sacrifice of love, that sacrifice of faith. *"...a man there was, though some did count him mad, the more he*

---

[48] Philippians 4:19

cast away the more he had." [49] That's always the way it is with God. Paul writing to the Corinthian Christians encouraged them to give generously. *"Whoever sows sparingly will also reap sparingly, and whoever sows generously will also reap generously."* [50] *"God is able to bless you abundantly, so that in all things at all times, having all that you need, you will abound in every good work...You will be enriched in every way so that you can be generous on every occasion, and through us your generosity will result in thanksgiving to God."* [51] Paul is saying that as you give in faith then everyone is blessed and God is glorified. One of the things which excites me at the moment in this fellowship is seeing more and more money and possessions and gifts flowing from person to person, family to family, household to household, and from us out to other needs outside our fellowship to other parts of the world and God's church in different parts of the world. It's wonderful when this happens because as the money flows like this from person to person,

---

[49] John Bunyan, (1684) *The Pilgrim's Progress*, pt. 2
[50] 2 Corinthians 9:6
[51] 2 Corinthians 9:8-11

household to household and out, everyone gets blessed. The person who gives gets blessed; the person who receives gets blessed. God is glorified. People are enriched in every way as we learn to be generous with the gifts that God has entrusted to us, and that really excites me when I see it happening. That's surely what the grace of God is like. It's never static, it's always flowing from person to person because God is teaching us to be men and women of faith, bringing us to the point where we have to trust him for everything in life, including our financial and material security. In a passage where Jesus taught about not being anxious for tomorrow, not being anxious for your life, not being anxious for your money, your possessions and so on, he says those familiar words which we often sing, *"But seek first his kingdom and his righteousness, and all these things will be given to you as well."* [52] And then he went on to say, *"Do not be afraid, little flock, for your Father has been pleased to give you the kingdom. Sell your possessions and give to the poor. Provide purses for yourselves that will not wear out, a treasure in heaven that will never*

---

[52] Matthew 6:33

fail, where no thief comes near and no moth destroys." [53] In other words as you give, as you have empty hands, it's your father's good pleasure to give you the kingdom. He is training us to be people of faith, who really do depend on him—not using that word faith as just a religious word—but so that it becomes a vital part of our life, depending upon him for everything. A sceptic once said, "Blessed are those who expect nothing, they shall not be disappointed." But we should be those who really expect God to work. There is a great deal of difference between those who believe that they believe and those who really believe. You can tell the difference between the two when we are put to the test; through times of financial hardship; difficulty; disappointment; illness or suffering. When we are put to the test it is then that we see if we are those who believe that we believe or are those who really believe and trust in God. Martin Luther one day met a peasant, a farmer who was very depressed. "Why are you depressed," he asked. "My house and my stocks have been destroyed by fire. I've lost everything. Life is no longer worth living." Luther

---

[53] Luke 12:32-33

asked him if he knew the Apostles Creed and replied that he did. Well say it then. "I believe...heaven and earth." Stop, he said. Say it again. "I believe..." Stop, he said. Say it again. "I believe..." Now, he said, if you really believe that, won't the mighty God, maker of heaven and earth, your heavenly Father, meet your need? So often faith is a cheap word on our lips. We say we believe but how far are we willing to trust our God in terms of even our material possessions and needs?

IT WAS A GIFT OF HERSELF

"...but she, out of her poverty, put in everything—all she had to live on." [54] This woman's gift was minute in financial terms, but it meant more to God than all the £10 and £20 notes, that had so ostentatiously been put in by the comparatively rich. Why? Because it was not only a gift of love and a gift of faith, but it was a beautiful expression of the gift of herself, of her whole life. During this series I have tried to be practical and down to earth in terms of giving, because there can be a kind of deceptive piety where we gladly and

---

[54] Mark 12:44

repeatedly offer to God the sacrifice of ourselves without giving to our neighbour sacrificially in their very real material need. The apostle John rightly exposes any pious talk that anyone might have along these lines when we're tempted to say that we love God but we don't love our brother. *"If anyone has material possessions and sees a brother or sister in need but has no pity on them, how can the love of God be in that person?"* [55] And the motivation for really expressing our love in practical terms is simply Jesus and the cross. *"This is how we know what love is: Jesus Christ laid down his life for us. And we ought to lay down our lives for our brothers and sisters."*[56]. Jesus supremely showed us the real meaning of Christian love when he gave himself and all that he had, even his own life, for ordinary; sinful; unlovely; rebellious; needy people. William Barclay once wrote "...people are always more important than things. If possessions have to be acquired, if money has to be amassed, if wealth has to be accumulated at the expense of treating people as things, then all such riches are

---

[55] 1 John 3:17
[56] 1 John 3:16

wrong."[57] The essence of being a Christian is love, and love means giving to God and giving to one another in love for God. At the service of Holy Communion we have the perfect example of this. At the offering of the bread and wine we say, "Receive the body of our Lord Jesus Christ which he gave for you and his blood which he shed for you. Remember that he died for you." There is the reality of his love. C.T. Studd, the wealthy England cricketer, Etonian aristocrat and Cambridge graduate, with everything at his feet, gave away his fortune and his life to Jesus Christ.[58] He said, "If Jesus Christ be God and died for me, then no sacrifice can be too great for me to make for him."

---

[57] William Barclay (2013) *Insights: Money: What the Bible Tells Us About Wealth and Possessions*, Saint Andrew Press

[58] CT. Studd emphasised the life of faith, believing that God would provide for a Christian's needs. His father died while he was in China, and he gave away his inheritance of £29,000, specifying £5,000 to be used for the Moody Bible Institute, £5,000 for George Müller mission work and his orphans, £5,000 for George Holland's work with England's poor in Whitechapel, and £5,000 to Commissioner Booth Tucker for the Salvation Army in India. Source: https://en.wikipedia.org/w/index.php?title=Charles_Studd&oldid=1078962224

I hope for many of us this will be the beginning of a fresh understanding, with practical action, about what Christian loving, giving and sacrifice are all about. The poor are always with us. They don't go away once this series is over. So may we increasingly bring gifts of love, gifts of faith, gifts of our very selves to the one who for our sake was willing to become poor that we might become rich.

Father, we thank you for this beautiful example of the poor widow who gave so little in one sense and yet so much and delighted the Lord Jesus when he was so tired and weary with this world. Father, we ask that our giving, whatever it may be (it may be quite small compared with others) but grant that it may be from a heart full of love; full of faith; an expression of our giving of ourselves to you, so that we too may delight the heart of Jesus. Grant that we may respond to his love as he has loved each one of us and given himself, broken his body, shed his blood that we might live. We ask it for his name's sake. Amen

Chapter 6
Q&As

1. IS IT RIGHT OR WRONG TO SAVE?

There's a tendency that we all slip back into simple rules and regulations, into law again. For example, is it right to save, or is it wrong to save? And if it's right to save, what proportion should I save, what proportion should I give? I can see behind these questions a lot of desire for fairly rigorous laws, rules and regulations. All the way along I've said that isn't New Testament Christianity at all. We're not under law, we're under grace. There are no answers to be given from the New Testament on that question, so, just turn for a moment to Acts 5:4,

> *Didn't it belong to you before it was sold? And after it was sold, wasn't the money at your disposal? What made you think of doing such a thing? You have not lied just to human beings but to God.*

This comes just after two tremendous passages in Acts 2 and Acts 4, when the early church had everything in common. They sold their land; they sold their possessions. They distributed them all as any had need. Then you have this tremendous judgement falling on Ananias and Sophia, not because they did not do that, but simply because they were lying to the Holy Spirit,

> *Now a man named Ananias, together with his wife Sapphira, also sold a piece of property. With his wife's full knowledge he kept back part of the money for himself, but brought the rest and put it at the apostles' feet.*[59]

Ananias was pretending he had laid everything at the apostles' feet. And Peter said, *"Ananias, how is it that Satan has so filled your heart that you have lied to the Holy Spirit and have kept for yourself some of the money you received for the land?"*[60] Now notice this next verse, *"Didn't it belong to you before it was sold? And after it was sold, wasn't the money at your disposal?"*[61] In other words, God does not impose rules and regulations, he gives us, in his love, freedom

---

[59] Acts 5:1-2
[60] Acts 5:3
[61] Acts 5:4

to respond to his love. He loves us freely; he wants us to respond freely. There are no rules and regulations, not even in this tremendous atmosphere in the early church where they were selling and going on selling their possessions. *"Didn't it belong to you before it was sold? And after it was sold, wasn't the money at your disposal?"* The problem was they had lied, not to each other but to the Holy Spirit.

In 2 Corinthians chapter 9, Paul is urging the Corinthian Christians to be "excelling in this gracious work" of generosity and really generous giving.

> *Remember this: Whoever sows sparingly will also reap sparingly, and whoever sows generously will also reap generously.*[62]

Each must do as they have made up their mind to do. Not reluctantly or under compulsion (from Paul or from anyone else) *"for God loves a cheerful giver."*[63] Remember that the word "cheerful" in the Greek means literally "hilarious giver", someone who just

[62] 2 Corinthians 9:6
[63] 2 Corinthians 9:7

roars with laughter as the £10 notes come flooding out. He loves someone who loves to give generously, cheerfully, hilariously. Therefore, you must do what you've made up your own mind to do before the Lord. There are no rules. There are no regulations on this. It is interesting that in chapter 8 verse 3, even when Paul is talking about the Macedonian Christians who are such a magnificent example,

> ...they gave as much as they were able, and even beyond their ability. Entirely on their own...

These are free will offerings, not compulsory laws. There is freedom about this. So, biblically, there is no answer to whether something is right or wrong. Practically speaking there are a whole variety of different circumstances, some people are single, some are married, some have dependants, and some don't have dependants. There are a whole variety of situations. Some are Christian partners of non-Christians, and they are in a particular category—they cannot just do what they would like to do. They have got to honour the marriage relationship. Therefore, you cannot say that this is right and that is wrong. One of the gifts of the Spirit is the gift of faith, and I take that to be not just saving faith, which we all have if we have faith in Christ at all, but a particular measure of faith given to some but not to everybody in the same measure. God does call out a George Müller; God does call out certain people to live by faith. God may call certain people to give up any idea of insurances or anything like that. But the fact that somebody is called out and may feel deeply convinced by God that is what their calling is, doesn't mean that is the first-class Christian life that everyone else ought to emulate. There are different gifts—faith and generosity are two of the gifts of the Holy Spirit. That is why, as I said right at the very beginning, we are from time to time to challenge one another, yes, to provoke one another to love and good works, but absolutely not to judge one another. What I do is before the Lord. What you do is before the Lord. But I suspect it will be very different. This is where we need to exhort one another, we need to challenge one another, but don't be under the law about it. Each one of us must do what we have made up our own mind to do before the Lord.

2. WHAT ABOUT HELPING THOSE SUFFERING IN OUR OWN COUNTRY?

Another trend is seeing our responsibilities too much in black and white, Here's an example, "While we should be really concerned about the people starving in other countries, shouldn't we also be just as concerned for people in our own country who are really suffering with such things as loneliness, violence, family break-down, poverty, sexual exploitation, mental illness, long-term unemployment and much more? Starvation kills but so does such things as suicide and cancer. I believe that if we neglect the problems at our own back door in favour of going all out for overseas aid, it will get worse. In some senses it is easier to solve problems in another country."

Well, in one sense that can be so, because it is easier to put some money in an offering for a country such as Yemen and you don't have to get involved with the people there in any depth. It is sometimes harder getting involved with those who are very close to you. "For me to love the world's no chore; my big problem is the person next door." Or whatever the saying is. I think this is putting it too much in black and white terms. In other words, there are vast areas of need everywhere and as a church we must be aware of the whole variety and range of needs. Certainly, there are people struggling here in York. In the very street in which you live I am quite sure there are people in need. But there are still 815 million starving people in different parts of the world. We can't just ignore that. We've got to try and widen our area of understanding when it comes to the needs here in York, in this country, overseas, everywhere. We've got to try and have a broader vision. Most of us tend to be very parochial and just exist in our own little patch. Well, God is the God of the whole world and increasingly our vision has got to widen so that we begin to see his concern, his agony in different parts of the world, although we can't be involved in equal depth everywhere.

3. RESPONDING TO LOCAL NEEDS

Another question is similar: "Isn't it more likely that we as God's people in York will be called upon to be discovering more effective ways of giving and ministering within the local body of Christ and to be meeting the needs of those non-Christians near at hand? And since we're not experiencing much evidence of God's power at work in our midst to meet those demands, when we are confronted by the huge needs of the third world, that has led to the overwhelming effect of making many of us feel thoroughly crushed." Well I know exactly what the writer is talking about here. In one way feeling at times thoroughly crushed, thoroughly frustrated and overwhelmed, is a very good, healthy thing. Just as at times we have to be reconciling people by taking hold of a person with one hand and taking hold of another person with the other hand and trying to bring them together, there is a measure in which we have to do the same reconciliation with emotions. We've got to enter into the grief and pain and anguish, the agony and crushing feelings that some people have at the same time knowing that in Jesus there is life and hope and joy and victory. And somehow bring the two together. If we're only crushed, we can't help. If we're only very triumphal Christians all the time, we're not really sensitive to those who are crushed. Emotionally we have to be in the position of a mediator almost at times. Therefore, it doesn't worry me too much if from time to time when most of us live a pretty comfortable sort of existence, we do just feel overwhelmed with grief and pain and the hopelessness of it all for so many in the world. Jesus was moved with compassion. It comes over and again in the gospels, about 7 times the word compassion is mentioned. The word compassion literally means "to suffer with" someone. You don't really have compassion for someone until you suffer with them, until in some measure you enter into their suffering. If they are crushed, in some measure you have to feel crushed with them. If they are lonely or in despair, in some measure feel that deep within your bones. It's not a bad thing to feel like that from time to time. It's part of the meaning of love. If we really open our hearts to love people, we are going to get hurt time and time again. Love makes us very vulnerable. The Prior of Taizé has said "to have opted for love, that choice opens in us a wound from which we never recover."[64] God calls us to love people, but it will hurt all the way along the line. Now let me stress that not every Christian can do everything, but together we should be increasingly concerned with a whole variety of needs here in York, in this country, the mission field and the developing world. That's why we need to work together; recognise; appreciate and support one another's different burdens. Some may have a tremendous burden for a developing country. Praise God for that and let them go on challenging us about that. We can't equally be involved in everything, but this is where

---

[64] Brother Roger of Taizé quoted in Quaker Friends Journal October 1st, 1981

the body of Christ begins to mean something. In some measure we should be concerned about what God is doing through his body in different ways, in different areas of need. So, let's not see our responsibilities as being either the developing world or here in York, but as a body we should be growing more and more concerned where there is need to be found in today's world.

4. How do I balance saving time and saving money?

This is a very practical question. Technology can save us a lot of time but there is a balance to be found somewhere. It's worth remembering that hi-tech gadgets consume vast amounts of the world's resources. Also, these gadgets are thought to be an important factor in the breakdown of relationships and families. It's very interesting that one list of the causes of family breakdown describes firstly: mobility, people moving from place-to-place job-to-job too quickly. Secondly, the depersonalisation of human beings in our high-tech society. We all become like machines. We lose our significance. Third is the sexual revolution. Fourth, affluence. Our materialistic culture practically eliminates the meaningful interpersonal relationships necessary for a happy home. Things, gadgets, tech, possessions—these are the centre of the home not people. So, we cease to communicate as people. The things have taken over. Relationships break down. Five, growing permissiveness in training children. Six, home entertainment channels, film. Their shallow portrayals of love and their addictive tyranny make an effective home life most difficult. Those are the six main reasons for the breakup of families. So, there is something to be said for tech but just watch out that they don't take the place of real relationships. Affluence does not mean happiness of course. I've sometimes quoted before Brian Clough who said "we drive the best cars, we live in the best hotels, we are the product of the best that a thousand years of civilisation can give us, but we are strained and we are tense and we never stop. It isn't my definition of a good life, but I don't know what is,"[65] You know, sometimes when we really work hard at simple living, it may take longer but you do things together very often. And that in itself is a very good thing. I am the

---

[65] The original source of this quote has not been found and therefore cannot be verified or properly attributed

world's worst person when it comes to anything practical. The number of times I have tried to do something in the home and the thing just breaks down and I have to do it again. I had a lot of fun working with a church member who is very gifted with his hands building a simple cycle shed which I couldn't have done in a thousand years, but working together we had a very happy, fruitful day which I remember vividly. We had an absolutely crazy day but a very happy day trying to find a second-hand engine for our VW when it blew up. We scoured all the scrapyards of Yorkshire and eventually found one in Pontefract where we found a greasy horrid engine which we dragged all the way back to York, sat on the lawn in the drizzling rain trying to clean the whole thing up, took it down to the garage who said that the whole thing was useless anyway. But it actually was still a very happy day doing something together! It wasn't a very good justification of our time but at least we had real fellowship together at a level which wasn't just planning the next service. When you try and do things like that, you sometimes enter into a new relationship which we otherwise miss out on because we're going so fast, doing the thing which seems to be the most obvious to save time. Well, sometimes instead of consuming more time and leaving less time for people, it works the other way round. I remember, for example, when we first moved into St Cuthbert's and we decorated the church, it was almost like a fortnight's mission for the whole congregation, just by working together. Practical work together was a wonderful time spiritually as well as every other way and deepening friendships and really getting to know one another well. But there is a balance here, so don't just go for the high-tech or disposable solution. It may be right, but it may not be right if you want to develop relationships.

5. Is the value of a secular job just to support others for fulltime Christian work?

> *...whatever you do, whether in word or deed, do it all in the name of the Lord Jesus, giving thanks to God the Father through him.*[66]

Everyone is in fulltime Christian work, in the right sense of that work. Everything that you do should be done for the Lord, whether it's in a factory, in a kitchen or an office, it can be fulltime for the Lord. "Do

---

[66] Colossians 3:17

everything as unto the Lord." That's what it ought to be. However, somebody has asked this: "If Christians group together in households, sharing and living off very little like you suggest, don't we risk becoming a sort of counterculture for many, opting out of the world altogether? I found that moving in such circles alienated me from non-Christian friends." Well, that can certainly happen. But I think we need to ask ourselves, and this is where everyone is different, what Christian ministry has God called us to? For example, a few people here, just a few people, have been called to the ministry of teams, the kind that went across to Belfast recently. Now it would be impossible to do that unless supported by several households. I've been longing to work with a team from our own congregation, having gone with the FisherFolk[67] on several missions. Obviously, it makes

---

[67] U.K. Christian music group comprising members of the religious 'Community of Celebration', based in the '70s in Coventry and Yeldall Manor, later Post Green and the Isle of Cumbrae, Scotland. The community was founded in Houston, Texas, U.S.A. by Rev. Graham Pulkingham. Their missionary worship tours were an early part of the 'Charismatic Movement' within liturgical Christianity. The FisherFolk grew into two touring teams. One team in Yeldall Manor then Post

more sense going with members from the same body of Christ, so that we can work together and train together. We at times are very humbled indeed by simple team visits across the region. What a blessing those visits seem to be to people, and therefore that is part of our ministry of encouragement, a certain ministry given to a few people maybe, but a ministry of encouragement that is very much needed today and hopefully which will spill out into more vital, joyful, loving Christian witness where people live, worship and work. It's only one form of Christian work but it's an important form. Now that's impossible without households. And if you feel that households cut you off from the world, let me remind you of the actual practice of some of the households of Houston, because they were faced as a large white-collar congregation with a Black community of 7000 people in high-rise flats. How do you get across to people living there with the gospel? Do you go around putting

---

Green, who did ministry to U.K. churches. And the other an international team based on the Isle of Cumbrae travelled as far away as Australia, New Zealand & South Africa. Later they returned to the USA to Colorado, and are now based in Aliquippa, PA

tracts through letterboxes? Well, they were able to set up a small medical clinic offering free medical help. After a time, they were able to have in that medical centre a hundred workers, including 4 full-time doctors and 12 part-time doctors. About 100-200 patients are served every day, all offered free treatment. The reason why free medical service is offered is that most of the workers, 80 out of 100, live in extended households. It's the only way they can do it. They therefore have minimal living expenses and have the financial, physical and spiritual support of those households. It's not aggressively evangelistic but when people come to the clinic, they sense the love of God there and many of the patients ask to be prayed for before they leave. Now that to my mind is an effective work made possible by households. The fact that you come together in a household doesn't mean that you just separate from the world. It may give you an entrée into a certain section of society that you would not otherwise have. I don't think our households have developed anything remotely to that extent but that is the vision behind them.

6. Aren't we getting too "good works-orientated" by focussing on giving and the needs of the developing world?

"It's not necessarily the wrong emphasis, we do need new challenges certainly, but going alongside this do you not feel there is an increasing need to be expounding the resources and the riches in Christ in greater detail? Isn't more of a balance required?" Well, I would say, yes of course there is. But I think that overall in this fellowship we have quite a lot of the balance the other way round. We have renewal weeks, renewal weekends, and regular devotional times. We're constantly trying to remind people of our riches in Christ. This is the first time since I've been here, some 12.5 years that I've ever taken a series like this. Now I feel that a bit to my shame, because Jesus gave us not only a great commission to go and preach the gospel, but he also gave us a great commandment to go and love. The two go together. I think for too long we've gone for people's souls as it were, to win them for Christ, without really caring for them in all their many needs. Just for a sort time, we're looking rather hard at some of the more physical, social and other needs which we have often neglected in this fellowship. A balance is necessary, but I don't think that we can be said to have swung massively in the wrong direction on this. The impact of the early church was that they were so caring for people like the widows with all their needs, this was part of the total demonstration of a God who loved, a God who has given his own son, Jesus Christ.

7. WHERE CAN WE SEND THE MONEY?

Well, I could give you a few suggestions but I think the problem about that is just this: "if we are able to live more simply and release more money, can you offer any guidelines on the balance between sharing these resources within the fellowship and sending them elsewhere. How can they best be sent?" Well, again I don't think there are any simple answers. For many people, it might be right for regular giving to go through the church, gift-aiding if you possibly can. Apart from that, there are extra needs within the fellowship, extra needs in the local area, extra needs in the mission field, extra needs in the developing world. Therefore, ask God to guide you when you want to give a special thanks-offering, or when you feel a real burden for a specific need.

8. IS GIVING MONEY TO DEVELOPING COUNTRIES REALLY THE ANSWER?

Money is not the answer. If money is involved, it must be as part of something else. We have to get rid of the idea that our money can solve the problems of the developing world. That doesn't mean we should stop giving money. Tearfund [68] for example is very concerned about trying to help people to help themselves, to find some self-respect, to build their own buildings, to organise wells, irrigation, farming, and set up businesses. Not just giving handouts but trying to help them discover what life and employment is all about. So money in itself is not all the answer, but money through an organisation like Tearfund will be well used and won't be just pushing money into people's pockets.

9. SHOULDN'T WE TRY TO CHANGE THE STRUCTURES OF SOCIETY?

"Is it enough simply to cut down on meat or to have one less cup of coffee a day? Shouldn't we do something much more radical?"

---

[68] www.tearfund.org

I would say, yes that is terribly important, at all kinds of levels, local and national government, taking action, writing to MPs. William Wilberforce[69] had people working for a year or two collecting information about the conditions on slave ships. When he came to argue with the people who made decisions in government, he was able to bring up information and to raise questions at a level where people could not brush him off just as a preacher. Sometimes it's too easy not to do the thinking and the hard work. Not everybody can do that work, these things are highly complicated and where we know organisations or groups or individuals who are really involved in this, then maybe some of our giving needs to be directed in that way. At the same time, having said something about the structures of society, we must begin with ourselves, our personal lifestyle and our corporate lifestyle. Otherwise, there is no credibility at all to what we are saying. We can shout about this and that, but it really comes down to how we are really living. We need to be involved in things which are going to

---

[69] William Wilberforce, British politician, philanthropist and leader of the movement to abolish the slave trade 1759-1833

influence the community here. We need to pray for vision. "Many are the plans in a person's heart, but it is the Lord's purpose that prevails."[70] We need to know what his purpose is, what his vision is, what his mind is, and pray for very clear guidance as we get involved in these things.

May I encourage you to do some more reading. Read some of the minor prophets. See how they were consumed with the injustices of their day. Do read *Rich Christians in an Age of Hunger*[71] because it sets out the biblical principles behind this so clearly and so helpfully. Whatever our feelings might be about any of these particular suggestions, we need to come back to the principles and then apply them as best we possibly can, as honestly and openly as we can—to ourselves and corporately as a church—as we move forward together in some direction along these lines and try to help in more effective ways those in need both here and overseas. The biblical principles are vital. And if you still have that measure of frustration

---

[70] Proverbs 19:21
[71] Ron Sider, *Rich Christians in an Age of Hunger* (London: Hodder and Stoughton, 1990)

and confusion, well praise God for it. And I hope you won't lose it too quickly.

However, we aren't to feel guilty if we can't immediately do something. That is a very important point, because I think that often when you feel frustration you feel condemned at the same time. This is why I stress again and again that we need to find our security in the love of God. God loves us just as we are. He doesn't condemn us. We need to keep our hearts wide open to the love of God and wide open to one another. So, his Spirit will lead and guide us, not to feel under condemnation that we're not doing what we see to be desperately needed, but to be open to be moved and led step by step.

www.ingramcontent.com/pod-product-compliance
Lightning Source LLC
Chambersburg PA
CBHW072058110526
44590CB00018B/3227